5 Principles
for a
Successful
Life

5 Principles for a Successful Life

for a

Successful

Life

From Our Family to Yours

NEWT GINGRICH

AND

JACKIE GINGRICH CUSHMAN

CROWN
FORUM
NEW YORK

Copyright © 2009 by Newt Gingrich and Jackie Gingrich Cushman

Published in the United States by Crown Forum,
an imprint of the Crown Publishing Group,
a division of Random House, Inc., New York.
www.crownpublishing.com

CROWN FORUM with colophon is a registered trademark of
Random House, Inc.

Library of Congress Cataloging-in-Publication Data is available
upon request.

ISBN 978-0-307-46232-9

Printed in the United States of America

Design by Barbara Sturman

10 9 8 7 6 5 4 3 2 1

First Edition

For Robert and Maggie Cushman

And everyone involved with the Learn and Earn
Pilot Program in Fairburn, Georgia, and the
Learning Makes a Difference Foundation, Inc.

One of the most important documents in our nation's history, the Declaration of Independence, states:

> *We hold these truths to be self-evident, that all men are created equal, that they are endowed by their Creator with certain unalienable Rights, that among these are Life, Liberty and the pursuit of Happiness.*

The Declaration of Independence does not guarantee happiness, just the pursuit thereof.

Furthermore, the phrase "pursuit of happiness" came from the Scottish Enlightenment, the period of time during the eighteenth century that was characterized by great intellectual and scientific achievement. It did not mean hedonism or partying—it meant the pursuit of virtue and wisdom. People in that era thought that those attributes were the keys to lasting happiness.

Your job is to pursue *your* happiness.

Only you can see your dream.

Only you can live your dream.

Contents

Principle 4 : Enjoy Life 111

Principle 5 : Be True to Yourself 157

Why 5 Principles?

The number five is important. The idea that any one of us—or our children or grandchildren—can learn a finite number of things is important. We don't have to learn one hundred rules to live successfully, we simply have to learn five principles and live by them.

Success. We hear the word often, but what is the definition of success? If you ask five people to define success, you will get five different definitions. Many people strive for material success—large homes, expensive cars, and designer wardrobes. Others look to recognition, celebrity, or societal impact as a marker. Some view success from a much more personal perspective: being a good mother, father, brother, sister, or daughter.

Since this book is focused on helping you achieve success, you might wonder how we define it. We focus on the long-term effects of our actions. For example, are we making the world a better place for our children and grandchildren? To us, success means adding value to people's lives and making a difference in the world around us.

Each of us has to determine for ourselves how to define success in life. Americans tend to focus on achieving success, but we often forget to focus on what creates success. Success does not happen overnight, and it does not happen easily. But we believe that *everyone* can find a way to be successful. The outcome is simply a result of an ongoing process—learning to live successfully.

Together our family has found that by following five principles, anyone can improve his or her life and create success: Dream Big, Work Hard, Learn Every Day, Enjoy Life, and Be True to Yourself. We began brainstorming on writing a book about these ideas a few years ago, when Jackie's children, Maggie and Robert, began to ask questions. Questions about how their grandpa became Speaker of the House. We thought it might be best for them to understand the process and how it happened over time—not overnight. Our goal is for Maggie and Robert and you to understand that success is a process that involves a lifetime of learning about how to succeed.

While these principles might appear to be simplistic and easy, mastering them requires diligence and perseverance. The application of any one of them might result in progress, but the integration of all five can lead to stellar results. Believe us; we know that sometimes it's challenging to live by your principles. Do not deceive yourself; there will be occasions when you will fall short. But in the end, it's about picking yourself up and moving back to the path that you want to follow. If you focus first on these principles and your values, you'll always make the right decision and follow the right path.

Both of us have tried to follow these five principles throughout our lives.

We *know* they can have a positive impact on anyone willing to learn them and live them, and we want to share them with you.

In this book, we hope to provide you with a playbook for success. Not a guarantee, but a path to follow that will improve your odds. We have included quotes from many people who are successful in a variety of areas.

These individuals provide real-life examples of how they achieved success by following these five simple principles.

Our dream is that this book will inspire and encourage you to pursue your happiness and that you will enjoy it once you find it.

Newt Jackie

May 2009

Principle 1:

Dream Big

If you can dream it, you can do it.

—WALT DISNEY

$\mathcal{A}$s a young man, I planned on becoming a zoo director or a vertebrate paleontologist. Yet during one special weekend as a teenager, I learned a powerful lesson that sparked my dream of entering public office and becoming a leader of our nation.

It was 1958, I was fifteen years old, and we were living in Orléans, France. My father was a career soldier—an infantryman. He served his country in World War II, Korea, and Vietnam. He understood that freedom is not free. During our time in France, my father took me to Verdun. That battlefield had been the largest and bloodiest on the western front in World War I. While there, we stayed with a friend of my father's who had been drafted in World War II and sent to the Philippines, survived the Bataan Death March in 1942, and went on to spend three and a half years in a Japanese prison camp during World War II. During that weekend, between talking to my father's friend and learning about Verdun, I was immersed in stories of the human sacrifices that were made for freedom throughout both world wars. I learned that the freedoms we now enjoy and take for granted were paid for in blood. This truth became very real to me during those three days at Verdun.

The lesson from history is that it is possible for bad leadership to result in the collapse of seemingly invulnerable societies. I was shaken by the realization that countries can disappear with remarkable speed when societies and their cultural values collide.

As an American, I believe everything we hold dear— our freedom, our prosperity, and our safety—is very fragile. During that summer at Verdun, my father taught me that we desperately need leaders who look beyond the present, who understand the seriousness of the threats we face, and who are willing to commit themselves to finding solutions worthy of our challenges.

The ultimate fate of any free society rests with our elected political leadership, and I decided it was my duty to become one of those leaders. This became my goal, my mission, my dream. That lesson from Verdun never left me, and it was the reason I ran for office. I ran for Congress twice unsuccessfully, but I never gave up on my aspiration to serve the public because I remembered those who never gave up defending freedom with their lives. After two defeats I won election and achieved my dream of becoming a leader for America.

Newt

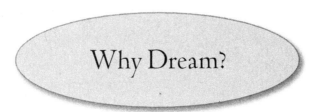

Why Dream?

Go confidently in the direction of your dreams.
Live the life you've imagined.

—Henry David Thoreau

Most of us dream when we are young. We dream about becoming fire fighters, police officers, ballet dancers, teachers, doctors, or astronauts. We do not consider whether realizing our dreams is probable or even possible. Instead, we let our minds wander to far-off places and enjoy our dreams.

At some point, often in middle school or high school, most of us are taught to give up our dreams and become "realistic." We are told that dreamers rarely amount to anything and that we need to learn to be practical. Limits and guidelines become more important than dreams and vision. We begin to focus on obstacles and probabilities rather than on goals and possibilities. As we start to grapple with the realities of adult life, our vision of the future narrows and dims. We abandon our childhood dreams and quit creating new ones. Our world becomes dull and routine, more obligation than fun. Many of us work for the weekends, counting the minutes until we can leave our jobs and entertain ourselves by watching television, playing video games, or shopping.

The truth is that dreams are essential, no matter what age we are—they help focus our energy on the future and keep us hopeful. To make a personal dream come true, you must set interim goals that bridge your current reality to that dream. Dreaming by itself will not make something happen. But dreaming—finding that picture and allowing its pursuit to motivate you—is key. It is the first step.

 Luis Haza *talks about the importance of always following your dream.*

~

As a child in my native country of Cuba, I dreamed of being an accomplished violinist and symphony orchestra conductor. By age twelve, my practice of music had led to a job in a professional orchestra, and I had made my conducting debut.

In pursuit of liberty, I left Communist Cuba and went to Spain, waiting for approval to come to the United States. While waiting, I practiced the violin seven hours a day.

My hard work in Cuba and Spain was the basis for opening doors of opportunity throughout my notable career in the United States. I dreamed big and worked hard, and that led me to realize the American dream.

Luis Haza is an accomplished conductor, violinist, and human rights advocate. He was born in Santiago, Cuba, and his commitment to freedom and human rights began at an early age, when his father was executed without trial because of his support for democracy. Haza's work has been recognized by President and Mrs. Clinton and Virginia governor Douglas Wilder, and he has received numerous honors, including the 2004 American Immigrant Achievement Award. The U.S. Congress flew an American flag over the Capitol in Haza's honor. In 1996, a scholarship was created in his name for the Kennedy Center Fellowship of the Americas, and Haza was one of the 100 Most Influential Hispanics in 1994. His performing career includes thirty years with the National Symphony Orchestra and twenty-five seasons as music director of the American Youth Philharmonic Orchestras. In 2005, Haza was appointed to the President's Committee on the Arts and Humanities.

Dream Big

If you would hit the mark, you must aim a little
above it: . . . every arrow that flies feels the
attraction of the earth.

—Henry Wadsworth Longfellow

When you dream, don't let practical considerations limit you: the bigger the better. Big dreams inspire you to action. They grab your imagination and fill your mind, consume your thoughts and lead you to act. Because they are hard to achieve, they provide you with a great sense of satisfaction once you have accomplished them. Remember that you will accomplish only as much as you dream you can—so if you want to accomplish big things, you'd better dream big.

Furthermore, it will take all of your energy, passion,

and time to achieve your dream. If you are going to work that hard, it had better be for a big dream.

Few men have dreamed bigger than Walt Disney. Disney set out to create a place where dreams reigned instead of reality, first through cartoons, then animation, and finally through Disneyland and then Disney World. Born in Chicago on December 5, 1901, he moved with his family in 1906 to Marceline, Missouri, then a town of 4,500 people where, according to Neal Gabler's biography, *Walt Disney: The Triumph of the American Imagination,* Disney recalled years later, "Everything was done in a community." It was this same small-town feeling that Disney re-created in 1955 in Disneyland's Main Street U.S.A.

It was not enough for Disney to dream simply of owning his own studio; he also dreamed of—and achieved—major advances in the art and impact of animation by doing things no one else was doing. Disney was the first to add sound and music to animation, the first to create a full-length animated film. Though he died in 1966, his dreams did not—his plans for Disney World came to fruition five years later, and his vision for Epcot Center was realized eleven years after that.

In *Walt Disney,* Gabler notes that Disney seldom

dabbled. "Everyone who knew him remarked on his intensity; when something intrigued him, he focused himself entirely as if it were the only thing that mattered."

Walt Disney's dream of making animated movies began unfolding after World War I, when he joined his brother Roy in California, and together they created Disney Brothers Studio. Their dreams and visions were contagious within the company, and biographer Gabler recorded the mood of the team. Ub Iwerks, a lead animator, recalled, "We all loved what we were doing, and the enthusiasm got onto the screen."

Our family often visits Disney World, creating lifelong memories. That same enthusiasm is felt by the millions of people who visit Disney World every year. Jackie has always had a place in her heart for the park that Walt Disney imagined and built:

I first visited the Magic Kingdom in 1978, after Dad won his first congressional election. On election night, when it became clear that he was going to win, at the victory party, he and my mother, Jackie Gingrich, announced to the crowd, and to my sister and me, that they were taking our family to Disney World.

I cannot remember if we flew or drove, but I do

remember staying in the Contemporary Hotel, with its indoor balconies and A-frame exterior. My favorite memories from that trip include driving a small speed-boat by myself (I barely made the age cutoff), riding the monorail, and playing in the game room.

Twenty-eight years after that first trip, our family returned to Disney World with my children. Watching the fireworks and listening to "When You Wish Upon a Star" with three generations of us at Disney World was an unforgettable experience.

For those who have not memorized them, the lyrics, as written by Ned Washington, include the following lines:

Anything your heart desires
Will come to you
If your heart is in your dream
No request is too extreme

Watching the fireworks and hearing the music, while recognizing that Disney World was created from one man's dream, reminded me that even big wishes can come true, and that big dreams can have an impact on the lives of millions of people.

* * *

Everyone can see what is certain and real, but only those who can imagine what *could be* have a chance to create and live their dreams. Those without a dream will have no reason to strive, work hard, or think of better days to come. People who dream big accomplish big.

Big accomplishments involve risk, and risk inevitably involves failure. It is the fear of failure that often stops people from dreaming big. They know that they can dream small and make something happen. It's the big dream that involves risk—but also the grandest rewards.

If you're lucky, you'll know someone who lives their dream—a dream others thought was impossible. Those who have attained the impossible dreamed the impossible. When you share your dream with these people, they'll encourage you. "Big men do not laugh at big ideas," David Schwartz says in *The Magic of Thinking Big.*

"The greater danger for most of us," said Michelangelo, "is not that our aim is too high and we miss it, but that it is too low and we reach it."

A big dream is a goal that will stretch you beyond your current capabilities. That is the point. Dream BIG.

Coach Lou Holtz *notes the importance of dreaming big as a step to success.*

⁓

Over the course of my lifetime I have discerned that there is not one single factor responsible for a successful life, but rather a combination of factors. I personally believe the desire to dream big is paramount to happiness and success. You can succeed when absolutely no one believes in you, but you have no chance to succeed if you do not believe in yourself. When you believe in yourself, then you will dream big.

During my early years I wanted little out of life: a car, a girl, $5 in my pocket, and a job in the mill. I thought, "Who could want more out of life?" Then I realized that the only things that will change you from where you are today to where you will be five years from now are the people you meet, the books you read, and the dreams you dream.

Everyone needs four things in their life or they will feel a hollow emptiness. Everyone must:

- Have something to do
- Have someone to love
- Have someone to believe in
- Have something to hope for, which is nothing more than dreaming big.

Coach Lou Holtz is best known for his eleven seasons as head coach of the Notre Dame football program. In addition to being the only coach in the history of college football to take six different teams to bowl games, win five bowl games with different teams, and have four different teams ranked in the final top 20 polls, Holtz has written three *New York Times* bestsellers and is considered among the greatest speakers in America. He has built his reputation as a motivator, a disciplinarian, and someone who relishes challenges and hard work. The 2008 Football Hall of Fame inductee also serves as a college-football studio analyst on ESPN.

Tavis Smiley *relates how to know when your dreams are big enough.*

When you work hard, your dreams do come true. But what do you do when your life exceeds your dreams? You dream bigger dreams. If people don't laugh at you when you share your dreams, then you're not dreaming big enough. Make them laugh. Dream big.

Tavis Smiley hosts the late-night television talk show *Tavis Smiley* on PBS and *The Tavis Smiley Show* distributed by Public Radio International. In addition to his radio and television success, Smiley has authored eleven books. Tavis also founded the Tavis Smiley Foundation, a nonprofit organization established to empower black youth. As a broadcaster, author, advocate, and philanthropist, Tavis Smiley is an outstanding voice for change.

 David Petraeus *follows the advice that his father gave him, to dream big.*

~

My father came to America from Holland at the beginning of World War II and served with the U.S. merchant marine throughout the war, eventually becoming a ship's captain. He always believed in the endless opportunities his adopted homeland offered. "Dream big, David," he told me when I was young. "As long as you work hard, you can be whatever you want to be." My father's advice has guided me through four years at West Point and thirty-four more in the army, and I, in turn, have passed on his wisdom to my two children, who are now realizing dreams of their own.

General David H. Petraeus is the commander of the United States Central Command. He previously served for more than nineteen months as the commander of the Multi-National Force–Iraq. Prior to these assignments, he commanded the U.S. Army's Combined Arms Center, the Multi-National Security Transition Command–Iraq, and the 101st Airborne Division (Air Assault).

Patrick Kerney, *defensive end for the Seattle Seahawks, provides us with an example of how falling short of a big dream set him up for success.*

~

D ream big: I couldn't agree more with this principle. It's not that I dreamed of being a professional football player ever since I could walk. Truth be told, I almost gave up football in tenth grade so that I could focus on ice hockey. It turned out that hockey wasn't my calling, and I originally went to the University of Virginia to play lacrosse. Through all these different turns in my athletic road, I always kept the same big dream in mind: perfect greatness.

Whether it was ice hockey, lacrosse, wrestling, or football, I always pictured in my mind what perfect greatness looked like on the field, in the weight room, running sprints, eating properly, and so forth. This vision has kept me very focused for a long time while I inch closer and closer to a level of perfect greatness that neither I, nor anyone else, will ever achieve. It is simply a compass to pull me back on the right road when my many human imperfections start to make me swerve off course.

Patrick Kerney is a Pennsylvania native, a University of Virginia graduate, and a first-round draft pick of the Atlanta Falcons in 1999. Kerney was recognized as the Falcons' Defensive MVP in 2002 and the Most Inspirational Player in 2004. He plays defensive end for the Seattle Seahawks and was named to the Pro Bowl in 2004 and 2007.

Your Dream and Only Yours

I dream my painting and paint my dream.

—Vincent van Gogh

Part of the challenge is for you to determine which dreams are meant for you, and you alone.

It is true that many times our dreams are influenced by others—our parents, siblings, grandparents, teachers, employers—and that is fine. While others may influence your dreams, however, only you can create them. After all, only you know what really makes you excited and ready to work hard.

One of the most difficult parts of dreaming big is making sure that the big dream is your dream and not someone else's. This becomes more important as you begin to craft how to cross the bridge from your current reality to your dream. If the big dream is *your* dream, it will test your talents and appear formidable, but it will be within your power to attain.

Your big dream will be in an area of your life where you have talent and interest. Talent is an important element because it is unique to you and provides you with the ability to perform better than others in the same area. A genuine interest is important too because it allows you to be passionate about your dream rather than trying to make yourself work toward a goal that doesn't interest you. Very few of us have the discipline to become masters in an area we dislike. Choose a dream that fits *your* passion.

Remember, however, that even though a dream draws on your talents, it is not a big dream if it is easily achieved. In *If You Want to Walk on Water, You've Got to Get Out of the Boat,* John Ortberg writes that the first response to a God-sized calling is often fear. "Where God calls, God gifts. It does mean, though, that natural talent alone is not enough to honor a calling from God. I will need ideas, strength and creativity beyond my own resources to do what God asks of me."

The American playwright and essayist Arthur Miller referred to the importance of matching your dream to your talents. "It's the lifeblood of a person, the song that her heart longs to sing, the race that his legs are born to run," he wrote. "There's an electricity associated with giftedness. Give a person a chance, and he'll jolt you."

We all have God-given talents. Each person is different from every other person, not only because of his or her external attributes but also because of his or her innate talents and interests. While your neighbor's dream might be appealing, in the end it will not work for you because the dream will not fit your own unique talents and interests.

Even if you were somehow able to achieve someone else's dream, you would not enjoy it as much as you would if it were your own. More important, you would miss out on the chance to pursue the dream that is yours alone. This dream is not only a gift, but a responsibility as well. If you do not follow your dream, who will? No one. It's yours to achieve.

In their *New York Times* bestseller *First, Break All the Rules: What the World's Greatest Managers Do Differently*, Marcus Buckingham and Curt Coffman discuss the differences among skills, knowledge, and talent. Knowledge is defined as "what you are aware of . . . factual knowledge—things you know," and experiential knowledge as "understandings you have picked up along the way." These are items that can be learned. Think of this as information that can be transferred to another person. Skills are the how-tos of a job. "They are the capabilities that can be transferred from one person to another." Skills can be broken down into steps and taught as a process of steps—like a PowerPoint presentation.

Talent is unique to each person. According to Buckingham and Coffman, great managers define talent as "a recurring pattern of thought, feeling or behavior that can be productively applied." This use of talent provides intrinsic satisfaction when the talent is utilized. "When people use their talent, they achieve satisfaction from the process—a great accountant feels thrilled when the books balance."

Talent can lead to feeling confident in forming and expressing strong opinions, reveling in confrontation, and paying attention to details. What we often think of as personality quirks or oddities are really the things that make each of us different. The key is not to gloss over them but to determine how to put these differences to their best use.

Talent can be overlooked. Instead of recognizing our talents for what they are, we sometimes assume that if an activity is easy for us, then it must be easy for everyone. In fact, if you find something is easy for you, you've probably found a talent. If you are struggling in a particular area, don't be discouraged. Instead, look in another area—your talent lies somewhere else. Listen to others when they tell you that you have a talent—they are usually right and are there to assist you in determining what you are supposed to do with your life.

Jackie often thanks a friend of hers who encouraged her in the early stages of her writing career. She told Jackie, "You have a gift; you have to use it." This often made the difference for Jackie when she was struggling with whether to give up or continue to work on her writing. Jackie thinks of her friend as her angel—sent to give her encouragement when it was needed. Be on the lookout for your angels.

We all can listen to that small, still voice inside of us that plants the seeds of creativity, and all of us can make a difference in this world.

Jim Loehr, *cofounder, chairman, and chief executive officer of the Human Performance Institute, knows the importance of big dreams that apply specifically to you. He incorporated that understanding into sport psychology, an area of expertise that he helped create.*

~

At the age of thirty-four, I had become chief psychologist and executive director of a large community mental-health center system that served an 8,600-square-mile area of southern Colorado. After serving four years in that position, I resigned to pursue a career path that didn't exist yet. When I made the announcement to the center's twenty-three-member board of directors that I was leaving to pursue a career in sport psychology, they were concerned that I had lost my mind. Somehow the dream of combining my love of psychology with my love for sport completely consumed me. The dream was intoxicating and so was the work, in spite of all the struggles and difficulties I faced in launching my new career.

Pioneering a new field required endless hours of hard work and focused effort. I've never regretted the decision for a moment. The last thirty years have been fulfilling beyond words. The Human Performance Institute, which I cofounded and for which I serve as CEO, is the complete realization of my dream of merging psychology and human performance. Without a big dream, without a willingness to work as hard as it took and the commitment to enjoy every minute of the struggle, none of the contributions we have made would ever have happened.

Dr. Loehr is a world-renowned performance psychologist, author, and developer of the ground-breaking Energy Management training system. He has appeared on NBC, CBS, and ABC, and has been featured in leading national publications such as *Newsweek, Time,* and *Fortune.* Dr. Loehr has a master's and a doctorate in psychology, serves on several prestigious scientific boards, and has worked with hundreds of world-class performers in the arenas of sport, business, medicine, and law enforcement.

Turning a Goal into Reality

A goal is a dream with a deadline.

—Napoleon Hill

Once you have a big dream that applies specifically to you, the next step is to determine how to turn that dream into reality. This requires attaching a deadline to your goal, creating steps to make it happen, and moving forward.

These steps require that you be very specific about the goal—what do you want to achieve, how can it be measured, and by what specific deadline do you want to reach this goal?

Instead of "It would be nice to have more Republicans in the United States House of Representatives," a clear goal was "We will attain a Republican majority in

the United States House of Representatives in 1995."
The 1994 elections resulted in a net gain of 54 seats in
the House of Representatives and a Republican majority
of 230 members of Congress versus 205 Democratic
members of Congress. Without the big dream spelled
out in the Contract with America, this would never have
happened.

Once identified, this big dream was broken into
smaller, achievable steps. Instead of being overwhelmed
by your big dream, create smaller activities with their
own measurable, incremental goals. A mile is 5,280 feet
and can be walked only by taking one step at a time.

These same steps of defining measurements and following a timeline work in everyday life as well as in national politics. Jackie's story about walking a marathon
with her sister, Kathy, illustrates this point:

*About 46 million adults and 300,000 children in Amer-
ica have been diagnosed with arthritis, the nation's leading cause of disability. My sister, Kathy, is one of them.*

*More than twenty years ago, when she was in her
twenties, Kathy was diagnosed with a particularly severe form of the disease, rheumatoid arthritis. For years
she struggled to find the correct medication, regimen,*

and health plan. Just a few years ago, her joints were swollen, she could not lift her arms above her head, and she found her daily walks on the beach in Florida, where she lives, taxing.

There were days when Kathy could not get out of bed without assistance. And days when she lay in her bed and wept from the pain. About six years ago, she started taking a new drug, which has arrested her disease and given her a new lease on life. By focusing on what she can control—strength, flexibility, nutrition, lifestyle, and working with a personal trainer—Kathy has become stronger and increased her range of motion. These days, she has resumed her walks on the beach near her house.

Now, Kathy states, "I don't think about it [having arthritis] except when I see someone else is in pain or hear their story, because of the gift of modern medicine."

In early 2007, Kathy and I decided to participate in the Arthritis Foundation's Joints in Motion program, which required that we cover 26.2 miles on foot. This was quite a stretch for both of us. I had completed the New York Marathon in 1993 but was no longer running, or even walking, long distances. Kathy was taking her daily walks but rarely exceeded four miles at a *time. Still, we knew that the goal of raising awareness and money for arthritis would provide us with the necessary drive.*

We decided on the goal of completing the Athens, Greece, marathon, which is held every fall. After all, since Athens is the birthplace of the marathon, it seemed to be a fitting location. Our dream of walking a marathon now had a deadline.

Our team, which we initially named America to Athens for Arthritis (A2A4A), included Phyllis Head, one of Kathy's closest childhood friends; Jeanne Cadwallader, a neighbor of Kathy's; Cynthia Counts, my great friend and running partner; and me. We created our own mantra, WALK ON!, which was intended to reflect our team's goal of moving forward with purpose.

When we began, several team members were nervous and hesitant about getting involved in fund-raising, but we were pleasantly surprised with the process. "In pursuit of fund-raising, I have reconnected and caught up with lots of old friends," Cynthia said, "and have heard numerous inspirational stories about others with arthritis." Jeanne said she was "thrilled with people who are making contributions, coming from unexpected places, in unexpected amounts."

While training, we changed our team name to America to Anywhere for Arthritis (A2A4A), not only reflecting our passion for raising awareness and money for the Arthritis Foundation but also capturing our spirit of adventure.

We left for Athens with more than $35,000 in donations for the Arthritis Foundation.

Marathon day started with a 4:30 A.M. wake-up call. As walkers, we were to begin two hours ahead of the runners. Our team got onto a bus at 5:15 A.M. and traveled to Marathon to begin the marathon at 6 A.M.

The start went well. The weather was perfect, high sixties, overcast with an occasional drizzle. About six miles into the marathon, we decided that coffee was in order, so Cynthia and I ran ahead to find a coffee shop. We received a few odd looks as we asked for coffee and wedding cookies, but the coffee was the best we drank the entire trip, and the cookies kept up our blood sugar.

After our coffee run, Cynthia decided to run the rest of the way, and she charged ahead. The rest of us walked on.

About eleven miles into the marathon, we were overtaken by the lead runners, whose pace—faster than five minutes per mile—was one I would not have been able to sustain for even a mile. The eventual winner, twenty-nine-year-old Kenyan Benjamin Korir Kiprotich, finished the course in 2 hours, 14 minutes, and 40 seconds. When he finished, we were four hours into our walk, just beyond the halfway mark.

At one point, we were passed by a runner dressed in Trojan garb, complete with skirt, breastplate, helmet, and shield. We learned later that it was his eleventh year running in Trojan dress, an outfit that weighed 30 kilos (66 pounds).

We walked on.

Our Atlanta-based marathon trainer, the former Olympian Jeff Galloway, who had entered the event as a runner, passed us while we were entering Athens, more than 75 percent of the way to the finish line. He stopped for a few minutes, encouraged us to continue, and ran on.

We walked on.

As we entered the stadium that held the finish line, we were met by Cynthia, who had finished hours before us. I turned to Kathy, smiled, and said, "Nike!" (Greek for victory). The smile on her face was proof that she too felt victorious. A few minutes later—seven hours and forty-eight minutes after we had started—

Kathy, Jeanne, Phyllis, and I crossed the finish line to-gether. Our deadline had been met, and our dream had been achieved.

After all the donations came in, A2A4A had raised more than $42,000 for the Arthritis Foundation.

And we had formed an even closer bond of friend-ship and sisterhood.

We decided to make the marathon adventure an annual commitment. In 2008, we walked the Dublin Marathon, added three new team members, and raised more than $65,000 for the Arthritis Foundation.

Walk on!

Create a deadline once you have a dream that you know is yours, and yours alone. Determine when you will start working to achieve your dream. When an obstacle comes up, which it will, don't look at it as an end to your dream, but as a detour to be navigated, as a problem to be fig-ured out and tackled.

Your dream—your goal—should not change, but your path to achieve the goal may change many times. Keep your goal and timeline in sight, and move forward with the flexibility to shift to whichever path moves you for-ward the fastest and with the least resistance.

After identifying your big dream and turning it into measurable goals with deadlines, put them in a place where you will see them daily. This will remind you of where you are headed and allow your subconscious to continually be working on ways to help you achieve your goal. U.S. Olympian Michael Phelps kept a list of his goals next to his alarm clock so he would see them every day. He won eight Olympic gold medals at the 2008 Summer Olympics, setting a new record for gold medals in one Olympics, and has fourteen career Olympic gold medals.

Once you have your dreams identified and listed in a place where you'll see them often, it is time to begin working hard to make them come true.

Alan Colmes *talks about the importance of turning a goal into a reality.*

~

I've always dreamed big. When you have a sense of purpose, a mission in which you truly believe, dreams have a tendency to fall into place.

But you can't just dream in a vacuum. All the principles work together. Dreams don't come to fruition without putting in the work.

I dreamed of being a broadcaster ever since I was a child. I received a tape recorder one Hanukkah and began doing radio shows that I'd play back for my friends. It was just a dream that I'd actually do it for real. But I put in the work (often for low pay) because I loved what I did. My first job out of college was at a small radio station in Rhode Island so I could do what I loved no matter where and no matter for how much money. But I worked hard, learned every day, made the most of what

I had, and stayed true to what I believed and who I was, always keeping the dream in my vision and in my heart.

That, in and of itself, is success. It's not how much money you make or how many accolades you receive. If you dream, work, learn, and enjoy, all while being true to your inner core, you have already achieved success— the best kind of success, in that no one can take it away from you.

Alan Colmes joined Fox News Channel in 1996 and served as the liberal counterpart to Sean Hannity in *Hannity & Colmes* through 2008. His interviews include many influential political figures. Most recently, Colmes returned to late-night radio as the host of *The Alan Colmes Show,* which is syndicated by the Fox News Channel.

Principle 2 :

Work Hard

The dictionary is the only place where success comes before work.

—VINCE LOMBARDI

I first learned about working hard from my Uncle Cal (Calvin Troutman). He and my Aunt Loma helped raise me when I was very young. They lived in the country, and I loved playing and walking around their land. Uncle Cal worked very hard at building roads. When he was home he was constantly doing things around the house, and when it got dark he would sit in a chair and read. He loved Louis L'Amour novels about the West. I got some of my love for reading from Uncle Cal.

He and Aunt Loma always said that you can do anything you put your mind to, but you have to be ready to work for it. Their own lives had been improved by constant hard work. They simply took it for granted that that was the way life was, having grown up in very demanding times: if they did not cut wood, there would be no fire in the cast-iron stove; if they did not can food, there would be slim pickings in midwinter and their diet would suffer. They knew that their limited income could lead to a much better quality of life if Loma sewed and knitted and Cal did practical work to improve the house. The result was a focus on daily steady work, an ethic that they passed on to me and that has stayed with me to this day.

My conclusion is that if you dream big, you have to be prepared to work hard to have any hope of achieving your dreams.

Newt

Why Hard Work?

*Patience and perseverance have a magical effect before
which difficulties disappear and obstacles vanish.*

— John Quincy Adams,
the sixth president of the United States

When you really have a big dream, it is in the fore-front of your mind at all times. You can't shake it. It is not just an idle wish, interesting or desirable, for money or fame. It's a goal you want to achieve for its own sake. This desire pushes you to work a bit harder than those who pursue dreams only for the immediate benefits.

Desiring your dream helps you put in that extra thirty minutes after practice, when the rest of the team is resting, and drives you to read about technique and tips before bed at night.

When Walt Disney decided to focus on animation, he worked every night in his garage, which served as the animation studio, long after everyone else had gone to bed. As Roy, his brother, recalled in Neal Gabler's biography, "Walt was out there, puttering away, working away, experimenting, trying this and that."

Disney doubtless discovered that working hard toward a goal stops being a burden and transforms into a way to fulfill your dream. The vision of your dream in your mind becomes so focused that the hard work is no longer *hard*. When you can imagine your dream being realized, it is easier to work a bit longer.

John "Jack" Horner, *an*

American paleontologist who advised on the Jurassic Park *movies, recalls that he had a firm handle on his dream from an early age and worked hard to make it a reality.*

~

When I was a little boy, I wanted more than any-thing to be a dinosaur paleontologist when I grew up. I wanted to find dinosaurs, dig up dinosaurs, and study dinosaurs. Many people, like my teachers, thought that was a goofy idea, because they didn't think I was smart enough to be a scientist. But I didn't let other people's ideas bother me. I believed in myself. I worked very hard, and I studied books about rocks, and about dinosaurs, and about biology. I even learned how to find dinosaur fossils. And it worked, because now I'm a dinosaur paleontologist.

John R. "Jack" Horner is the director of the largest dino-saur field-research program in the world. He and his team have made fascinating dinosaur discoveries and have named several new species. Upon receiving an honorary doctorate from the University of Montana, Horner went on to publish more than 150 professional papers, 7 popular books, and more than 100 popular articles. Horner was also the technical adviser for Steven Spielberg on all of the *Jurassic Park* movies and has worked with the National Geographic Channel and the Discovery Channel. Currently, he is the Ameya Preserve Curator of Paleontology at the Museum of the Rockies in Bozeman, Montana, and Regents Professor of paleontology at Montana State University. He is also a senior research fellow in the Department of Paleobiology at the Smithsonian Institution and an honorary research fellow with the Natural History Museum in London.

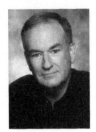

TV host and commentator
Bill O'Reilly *talks about how hard work produces success and keeps you at the top of your game.*

~

W hen it comes to my career in broadcasting, hard work and perseverance have been cornerstones of my success.

Broadcast news is so competitive that it is not enough to be talented. No, in order to rise to the national level, you have to produce more than the others who want your reporting or anchor slot.

The O'Reilly Factor has been the highest-rated cable news program for more than eight years. But I rarely rest. Each week I work about sixty hours—if you do the math, that's ten hours each weekday and five hours each Saturday and Sunday, on average.

I am the only national anchorman in the country who writes his entire program, including promotions. I do this because the audience is used to hearing my voice. Hiring writers would dilute the authenticity of the presentation.

Also, I select the subjects we talk about on *The Factor* because, well, they must interest me, since I'm the one doing a lot of the bloviating.

My father taught me to work hard and to never give up on a worthwhile cause. I learned the lesson well, and that's why you are reading these words today.

As the host of the highest-rated cable news show, **Bill O'Reilly** is probably the most controversial and frequently discussed TV analyst today. For more than seven consecutive years, no program has even come close to *The O'Reilly Factor*'s ratings. In addition to *The Factor,* O'Reilly finds time to do a daily two-hour radio show (heard on more than 400 stations), write a weekly column appearing in more than 300 papers, and write bestselling books.

Before joining Fox News in 1996, O'Reilly's national exposure began with CBS and ABC News. Along the way, he has gained a considerable following and earned numerous journalism awards, including three Emmys, as well as the 2008 Governor's Award in Boston.

O'Reilly was raised on Long Island and holds a bachelor's degree in history from Marist College, a master's in broadcast journalism from Boston University, and an additional master's degree in public administration from Harvard's Kennedy School of Government.

John A. Williams *of Williams*

Realty Advisors talks about the importance of working hard and why, even though his projects have already reshaped much of Atlanta, he wants to continue to work hard.

～

"Work hard" was drilled into me from my early childhood. I had an *Atlanta Journal* paper route at the age of ten. At that time, I was the youngest person to ever be given a route for the paper. A year later, I picked up a second route and was the youngest person to have two paper routes.

I still remember walking the streets, no matter how cold, no matter how hot, to collect the $1-per-week fee for subscriptions. There was never any time through high school or college that I did not have a job. Frankly, I would have been lost without the opportunity to work.

My mother pushed me to excel. She told me more often than I care to remember, "Hard work killed no one; lack of hard work will certainly have bad effects." She was quite the "pusher." No grade was good enough;

no accomplishment was as good as it could have been. As tough as this might seem, these traits have followed me throughout my career.

I think in the business world I compete in, there are many people smarter than I, but luckily, most of them do not have the work ethic or commitment to excel that I do. To this day, I still work a sixty-hour workweek, I always work on Saturday, and I generally do two hours of paperwork at home each evening. Fortunately, I love to work, I love to excel, and I have an affliction called the Perfectionist Disease, all traits inherited from my childhood.

Because I enjoy working and excelling, I plan never to retire.

John A. Williams, CEO of Williams Realty Advisors, LLC, has directed and coordinated the development, construction, and management of real estate developments since 1966. Williams was the founder of Post Properties, Inc., and also holds interests in various other entities. The forty awards, honors, and medals Williams has received during his forty-two years of success in the industry include being named Entrepreneur of the Year by both Stanford Business School and Ernst & Young in 1990 and 1988, respectively. He also received the Mack Henderson Public Service Award in 2005 for his outstanding community leadership. Williams serves on the board of directors of the Atlanta Falcons, of which he is minority owner.

Daily Action

They who lack talent expect things to happen without effort. They ascribe failure to a lack of inspiration or ability, or to misfortune, rather than insufficient application. At the core of every true talent there is an awareness of the difficulties inherent in any achievement, and the confidence that by persistence and patience something worthwhile will be realized. Thus talent is a species of vigor.

—Eric Hoffer (1902–1983)

We know that it takes hard work to get ahead. But how do we put that knowledge into practice? Nothing is out of your reach if you work at it daily, but often the divide between what we could achieve and what we actually accomplish is enormous.

We can create habits that will carry us through. This approach is most effective when a goal can be broken down into a series of short and easy tasks. For example, we train children to complete certain tasks on a daily basis: brush their teeth, pick up their clothes, take out the trash. The more these chores become habits that happen automatically, without forethought, the more likely they are to get done.

Surprisingly enough, we've found this strategy also helps us accomplish larger goals over time. One of the biggest fears that many people have is speaking in public. Yet if you can become an effective speaker, it is one of the best ways to communicate and inspire people. The best way to become an effective speaker is to speak every day. After teaching college for seven years, running for office for six years, and serving twenty years in the United States House of Representatives, Newt is an accomplished speaker. However, he still practices every day, and has been practicing every day for more than forty years. Daily activity produces great results over time.

The formation of our character is based on how we have spent our time and where we have applied our energies. Becoming successful requires deciding where to focus our efforts. In other words, we have to set goals. Our goals determine what we think, plan, and do and will ultimately determine who we become.

Let's face it: this process is not accomplished overnight. In today's world of instant messaging and immediate gratification, we often forget that some things take time, practice, and patience to achieve. Aristotle had it right when he said, "We are what we repeatedly do."

A writer who does not write is not a writer, an actor who does not act is not an actor, and a painter who does not paint is not a painter. Once they stop practicing their craft, they can no longer lay claim to the title.

We normally view time as a straight line: yesterday, today, tomorrow. This lays out a steady path where time seems to be a set of discrete events. Work one day, relax the next; it doesn't really matter in the end. But such a view does not consider the value of the ongoing activities that we weave into our lives day after day.

For example, in the linear view of time, it would not make sense for a three-year-old to begin to play guitar and to practice every day, since his or her progress would be so incremental that it would hardly be noticed from one practice session to the next.

But if the toddler practices every day for a decade or two, he or she has a much greater chance of transforming into a world-class musician.

As Confucius said, "Men's natures are alike; it is their habits that carry them far." Begin to create a habit today that next year, or next decade, or next time the cicadas swarm, will set you apart. While you might not see the results at first, the actions begin to build on one another.

John Ondrasik, *lead singer of the band Five for Fighting, credits his mother for his success, saying, "I began playing guitar at the age of three, and my mother made me practice every day." While he did not enjoy the practice at that time, he learned that if he worked on songs he liked, the practice went faster and was even a little fun. What a great concept: making something that we do to get better (daily, repetitive practice) fun by incorporating things (songs) that we enjoy into our routine.*

I'm a firm believer in a good work ethic. As a member of the twenty-year-overnight-success club, I can attest to the cool reality that nothing comes for free. I once calculated my hourly wage as a singer-songwriter. From age fifteen until I secured my first record contract, I wrote thousands of songs (most bad). My economic return? A robust 3 cents an hour! To this day, I write a couple hundred songs per record to get ten I can live with. Very few people are blessed (or cursed) with prodigy talent. The rest of us do the best we can with what we've got, and work ethic, drive, and commitment usually make the difference. I may not know a lot, but I do know that if I'm not sitting at the piano searching, no hopes, dreams, or falling stars will lend me a song to sing along.

John Ondrasik is a singer-songwriter of the group Five for Fighting. He is known for crafting songs with material drawn from his personal experience with regard to love, war, culture, family, humanity, and morality. These songs include the hits "100 Years," "World," and "Freedom Never Cries." In addition to his musical accomplishments, John has made a personal commitment to causes that are important to him. In mid-2007 he launched a charity-driven website, whatkindofworlddoyouwant.com. It raises money for various charities when users view video clips provided by visitors of the site. The site's success has led to a recent collaboration between Ondrasik and the History Channel. He has composed soundtracks for many films, including *August Rush, The Sisterhood of the Traveling Pants,* and *We Were Soldiers.* Ondrasik also writes a regular hockey column for SportsIllustrated.com.

Jeb Bush, *former governor of Florida, understands the importance of undertaking daily actions that might appear to be small, but over time have great impact.*

~

A long time ago, my dad told me that Ben Franklin once said, "Little strokes fell great oaks." Over time, I saw how doing the little things right, over and over again, was a key to success. My dad has lived his life that way, doing the everyday things like being decent, showing integrity, and working hard, over and over again, and it has worked for him. I am striving to make it work for me.

Jeb Bush was the forty-third governor of the state of Florida, serving from 1999 through 2007. He was only the third Republican ever elected to the state's highest office and the only Republican in the state's history to be reelected. Currently, Bush is the president of the consulting firm Jeb Bush and Associates and serves on the board of several charitable foundations including Excellence in Education, the Foundation for Florida's Future, CASEnergy, Volunteer USA, and Our Pledge.

Comedian Jon Stewart *proves he is funny every day, even when providing advice and guidance.*

I have not necessarily been blessed with the most talent, brains, or height, but one thing I do believe in is hard work. Hard work is the magic elixir that allows one to develop competence. Not that I'm against sitting around, it's just that that has proven less helpful . . . speaking for myself.

Jon Stewart is one of America's top social and comedic figures. As host of Comedy Central's *The Daily Show with Jon Stewart,* his interviewees have included presidents Jimmy Carter, Bill Clinton, and Barack Obama, as well as Hillary Clinton, John McCain, Tom Cruise, and George Clooney. In addition to being the bestselling author of *America (The Book): A Citizen's Guide to Democracy Inaction,* Stewart is also the cocreator and executive producer of Comedy Central's Emmy Award–winning *The Colbert Report. The Daily Show* has received twenty-two Emmy Award nominations and won eleven. Stewart was named as one of the world's most influential people on *Time* magazine's inaugural Time 100 list.

Getting Up Again and Again

Understand that obstacles are just part of the game.

Whatever you imagine, you can achieve.

—Russell Simmons,

hip-hop musician and fashion mogul

So now you know you have to dream big, dream your dream, set a deadline, and work hard. Sounds easy, right? That part is, but you also have to be ready for the inevitable—failure.

Everyone fails. Failure is not unique or important; it's your actions afterward that will set you apart.

Perseverance—working hard over a long period of time—is a key to success. If you are leading a group toward a goal, it's extremely important that you display this quality, since nothing inspires people more than see-ing those above them working hard.

As you follow your dream, have faith that the ob-stacles you encounter are temporary. Soon after Jackie became treasurer and a board member of Genesis: a New Life (an Atlanta shelter for homeless newborn babies and their families), it was determined that the shelter needed to be relocated. A capital campaign for $5 mil-lion was kicked off. Many obstacles appeared during the eighteen-month campaign. The nonprofit was not well-known, its application for a bridge loan was turned down by a large bank, and at one point, outside consultants told the board that the money could not be raised. Dur-ing this process, neither Jackie nor the rest of the board members gave up. They had an unshakable belief that "we can't have a homeless homeless shelter," as Jackie put it. Construction for the new shelter began before the funds were raised. In the end, the money was found, renovation completed on time and on budget, and the children and families were relocated successfully.

In his book *Learned Optimism*, Dr. Martin Seligman, director of the Positive Psychology Center at the Uni-versity of Virginia, describes people who never give up after setbacks. They are those who say to themselves, "It was just circumstance, it's going away, and besides, there is so much more in life," he writes.

According to Seligman, you can learn optimism by changing the way you think about events and by not giving in to feelings of helplessness after facing failure.

Why is optimism important? "Optimists recover from their momentary helplessness immediately," Seligman says. "Very soon after failing, they pick themselves up, shrug, and start trying again. For them, defeat is a challenge, a mere setback on the road to inevitable victory. They see defeat as temporary and specific, not pervasive."

Newt relates this story about persistence:

As I have said before, "Hard work makes up for almost everything." There will always be those who want to give up—but you can't give up if you want to reach your goal. There are several examples of persistence in my career, but the one that most frequently comes to my mind is my running for the U.S. Congress from Georgia and losing in both 1974 and 1976 before winning in 1978.

In 1974, I ran for the first time. It was the year of the Watergate scandal. Every day the news for Republicans got worse. Finally President Nixon resigned. Then Pres-

ident Gerald Ford gave him a pardon. The country was enraged. I was running against the dean of the Georgia delegation and the fourth-most-powerful member of the Appropriations Committee. I had no personal money and was taking a leave of absence without pay from West Georgia College. After an exhausting year, I got 48.5 percent of the vote. In a terrible year I had lost, but I did well enough to have dignity and to consider running again.

I was all geared up to run for a second time and felt good about my chances to get that extra 1.5 percent. I will never forget standing in our living room drinking coffee at seven A.M. one Wednesday in April, watching the Today show: Governor Jimmy Carter came from behind to win the Wisconsin primary with the votes of rural dairy farmers who identified with this Georgia peanut farmer (albeit also a nuclear-engineering graduate of Annapolis). I suddenly realized a Georgia Democrat favorite son was going to be at the head of the other ticket. I would have to run for the entire year just to do well enough to survive and run a third time.

The 1976 campaign was probably my best campaign in twenty-four years of running for office. By Election Day, I was feeling optimistic. I went down to the Neva

Lomason Memorial Library, in Carrollton, Georgia, at about four in the afternoon to vote. Just ahead of me in line were four elderly people who had come from the nursing home to cast their votes for a Georgia favorite son. As I listened to them talk, I realized that they were voting to get revenge for Sherman's march through Georgia during the Civil War. What were the odds, I thought to myself, that they would split their ticket for a Yankee-born army-brat Republican? I suddenly realized it was going to be another very long night and I was probably going to lose again. I was right. I dropped from 48.5 percent to 48.3 percent.

My frustration peaked the following Saturday when I was sitting alone in my campaign headquarters reviewing the votes and trying to think of what we could have done differently. I suddenly realized that in my home county of Carroll I had literally gotten twice as big a share of the vote as President Gerald Ford had. He'd gotten 26 percent and I'd gotten 52 percent. I realized with a sense of finality that it was virtually impossible to more than double the votes of the leader of your own party. Once again it just was not my year.

If I had quit then, the Contract with America and the Republican majority would not have happened. My campaign treasurer and good friend, Dr. Wayne Brown, told me after I finally won on my third attempt that he had almost begged me not to run again. He was afraid that I would be humiliated and become a laughingstock. But ultimately, he was happy that he had not tried to talk me out of it.

Many other people would have given up before running a third time. It was hard for me to lose, hard to sit at the local diner at two or three in the morning with my family and friends and know that we had lost a close election—again. Even harder to go later that morning to the shift change at the Ford factory and shake workers' hands and, though we had lost, thank them for their votes. But that is exactly what our family did.

Just think of the times: the mid-1970s, with no national or statewide elected Republican in Georgia. In 1974, the Watergate scandal had tainted the hopes of many Republicans, and in 1976, Jimmy Carter, Georgia's favorite son, was running for president as a Democrat. He won, of course, and carried Georgia with an enormous Democratic turnout.

I had already been twice defeated, but instead of giving up, my wife (Jackie's mother) and I decided to take a year off from work, borrow money, and campaign yet again. The third time was the charm. We finally won in 1978 and were on our way to Washington. In this case, persistence paid off.

This is similar to what Walt Disney did after his first business failure. In 1922, Disney opened Laugh-O-Gram Studio in Kansas City, a venture that ended in bankruptcy slightly more than a year later. The business manager noted that even after the bankruptcy, Disney "was always optimistic . . . about his ability and about the value of his ideas and about the possibilities of cartoons in the entertainment field." Phineas Rosenberg, Disney's bankruptcy attorney, noted, "Never once did I hear him express anything except determination to go ahead." Imagine all the delights the world would never have enjoyed if he had given up on his dream when faced with what proved to be only a temporary failure.

If you give up, it is guaranteed that you will not reach your goal. Keep persisting, and your dream may come true.

Radio host Michael Reagan

relates his story on persisting through failure — in this case, getting fired.

~

In 1992, after being fired from KSDO in San Diego because Rush Limbaugh's star was rising, I decided to think big and start my own national radio talk show. I had no money but I did know a couple of people who had shown an interest in trying to syndicate me. So on September 7, 1992, seven months after being fired, I launched *The Michael Reagan Talk Show.* We had no money, and I had to drive from my home in Los Angeles to San Diego every day (262 miles roundtrip) to do my show from a borrowed studio. One day on the drive I called my mother (Jane Wyman) to ask for advice. I had no money coming in, my two children were in private school, and my wife, Colleen, was trying to do the best she could to keep our heads above water. In fact, we had qualified for the earned income tax credit. I was thinking big, but was it too big? Well, my mother gave me this advice: "Shut up, quit feeling sorry for yourself, and keep driving." When

I asked her why she would tell me such a thing, she responded, "Everyone has their dues to pay and you are no different because of your parentage, and someday, when you look back at this, you will feel proud that you followed my advice and shut up and kept driving without your mother's and father's help." Then she just hung up. Well . . . September 7, 2008, started my sixteenth year in syndication for a show that Rush Limbaugh's people said would never make it the first year. The lesson is Never Give Up Your Dream.

Michael Reagan, the eldest son of former president Ronald Reagan, is heard daily by millions of radio listeners on his nationally syndicated talk-radio program, *The Michael Reagan Show*, and can also be heard worldwide at www.reagan.com.

Prior to launching the national program, Reagan set world records in powerboat racing. His racing raised more than $1.5 million for charities. He serves on the board for the John Douglas French Alzheimer's Foundation.

He has authored many successful books, including his bestselling autobiography, *On the Outside Looking In,* and *The Common Sense of an Uncommon Man: The Wit, Wisdom, and Eternal Optimism of Ronald Reagan.* His latest book, *Twice Adopted,* is based on his personal story.

 *Diplomat* John Bolton *talks about how getting up and continuing to work hard after failure creates confidence.*

"Working hard" may not sound very enjoyable, but without it you are likely to accomplish very little. This is especially true if you didn't pick the right parents who were already highly educated, cultured, wealthy, and powerful when you came along.

For most of us, hard work means studying, preparing, and practicing until we get it right, which takes time and effort, and it can be discouraging when you stumble or don't immediately succeed. But real satisfaction comes when you master your task, realizing that you did it yourself, thereby gaining self-confidence to try something even harder the next time.

John R. Bolton currently serves as a senior research fellow at the American Enterprise Institute. Prior to his arrival at AEI, Bolton served as the United States permanent representative to the United Nations and as undersecretary of state for arms control and international security in the George W. Bush administration.

Political consultant James Carville *provides his take on why it is important to never give up your dream.*

All of my life, I wanted to be a political consultant. At age thirty-seven, single and unhappy with my job as a lawyer, I decided to follow my dreams. I had a very slow start and actually lost my first few races. At forty-one, I had no money, no job, and no health insurance. But the last thing that dies in somebody is a dream. Months later, I got a job working to elect Bob Casey for governor in Pennsylvania and the winning streak never stopped. I even helped get Bill Clinton elected president in 1992. Work hard and never let your dreams die.

James Carville is one of America's best-known political consultants. His most prominent victory was in 1992 when he helped William Jefferson Clinton win the presidency. Carville is also an author, actor, producer, talk-show host, speaker, and restaurateur. Carville's most recent ventures include hosting XM Radio's *60/20* weekly sports show and frequenting CNN as a political commentator and contributor.

Cheerful Persistence

Lay aside life-harming heaviness and entertain a cheerful disposition.

—William Shakespeare

Y ou often hear about the value of persistence, the claim that attitude is everything. But rarely is the phrase "cheerful persistence" mentioned. That's unfortunate because, once the two are combined, they form a concept that is almost unstoppable.

To persist, according to the Merriam-Webster online dictionary, is "to go on resolutely or stubbornly in spite of opposition, importunity, or warning." To be cheerful is to be "full of good spirits." Thus, the idea of cheerful persistence is to continue in the face of adversity (or, to be blunt, failure), full of good spirits.

If you think about it, you have four choices regarding how to act. You can be unpleasantly persistent, cheerful while surrendering, unpleasant while surrendering, or cheerfully persistent. It may be easier to break down the options—persistent versus surrendering, cheerful versus unpleasant.

Persistence requires forging ahead and working hard, not giving up at the first or second or even third obstacle, but relentlessly plugging away.

So how do you learn to be consistently cheerful? The first requirement is to learn to relax and accept that no one gets it right the first time. Accepting failure is an important part of learning to succeed. Once you have learned to relax and focus on each outcome as a learning experience, it becomes easier to be cheerful. Cheerfulness comes from within and is so powerful it can change the lives of people around you.

As Newt wrote in an op-ed for the *Weekly Standard* regarding the Great Communicator: "Cheerfulness can get almost anything done. One of President Reagan's great strengths was his commitment to big ideas and his willingness to remain cheerful no matter what the difficulties were. It made him likable and approachable and easy to support. Despite being the son of an alcoholic father, entering the job market in the Great Depression, and watching his career in movies fade out, Reagan remained a steadfast optimist. That disposition was a tremendous, politically potent change from the angry pessimism of traditional conservatism."

Newt has always believed in the concept of cheerful persistence, and in fact, he may have coined the phrase! Newt began to use the phrase routinely during the 1980s when he was working to build a Republican majority in the U.S. House of Representatives. "Remember, I thought we could be a majority. The Democrats didn't want us to be a majority, and most of the Republicans didn't want us to be a majority. We had a whole bunch of Republicans that said, 'Hey, we're going along. I like my chairman. We go golfing together. We're good friends.'

"And I was going around saying, 'No, we've got to beat these guys.' And we began recruiting younger members, and we had to coin the phrase 'cheerful persistence.' If you didn't persist, you couldn't get anything done, and if you weren't cheerful, people wouldn't work with you."

According to Jackie, her dad's own adoption of cheerful persistence came later when he began to fully incorporate the concept into his being:

So what about the cheerful part? Few people had ever accused Dad of being cheerful—many other things, but not cheerful. In fact, it is only in the past few years that he has been consistently cheerful. It became apparent to me sometime after he resigned as speaker in 1998. As I watched him on Fox News, I noticed his demeanor had changed. No longer did he appear defensive; instead, he appeared the statesman, projecting ease, confidence, and, yes, cheerfulness.

The ability to persevere with cheer is indicative of having faith in your ultimate success. If you believe that, then any failure is temporary, simply an opportunity to learn before resuming forward motion.

So the next time you face an obstacle, face it with cheerful persistence: have the willingness to try again and again while being full of genuine optimism and hope. With this renewed optimism, you will be ready to learn and make your way toward your goal.

Cofounder of The Home Depot,
Bernard Marcus *tells about the impact his mother had on his approach to life, and his years of long hours and hard work, with his belief that over time they would pay off and lead to his success.*

~

My mother believed that America was the golden land, and whatever you put your mind to, you could achieve. She told me you had to work hard to be successful.

Working hard and taking responsibility for your own actions make it easier to create something substantive in your life. In the atmosphere of a free-enterprise system, you can achieve and be successful. But you have to work hard and put your brains, heart, and soul into it. If you're looking for a handout, it just doesn't happen.

Bernard Marcus is cofounder of The Home Depot, Inc., the world's largest home-improvement retailer. He is the creator of the Marcus Foundation, a charity organization that focuses on Jewish causes, children, medical research, free enterprise, and the community. The Marcus Foundation is a major sponsor of the Georgia Aquarium; the Marcus Institute, which provides programs for children and adolescents with disorders of the brain and their families; and Project S.H.A.R.E., dedicated to ensuring that members of the military and veterans get medical assistance without financial constraint; among many other charitable organizations.

One of America's leading airshow pilots, Jill "Raggz" Long *talks about the importance of persistence in attaining your dream.*

~

People often ask what the motto "Live life on the ragged edge . . . and follow your dreams" is all about. I believe that every truly great accomplishment at first appears to be impossible. Believe in yourself, never stop learning, and never ever listen to those who tell you it can't be done. Everything is possible if you are willing to work hard, stay focused, and never take no for an answer.

Lt. Col. Jill "Raggz" Long inspires audiences in the tens of thousands each year as one of America's leading female airshow pilots—that is, when she's taking time off from her duties in the air force. She was the only woman to cross-train into the A-10 Thunderbolt (a.k.a. "Warthog") after six years in the KC-135 and has accumulated more than four thousand flight hours and flown in fifty combat missions. She is currently "hanging chocks" in Aviano, Italy, as the 8th air support operations squadron director of operations.

Ricardo González, *founder and president of Bilingual America, relates how persistence and focus on relationships— skills learned from his parents—have helped him to create a successful business.*

M y father was one of twenty-seven children from the mountains of Puerto Rico and my mother was an orphan from the hills of Kentucky. Dad came to the United States with a ninth-grade education and spoke no English. Together they started and grew a very successful restaurant out of a converted horse barn. I learned that in life, no matter how high the walls, you can succeed if you work hard and treat people well.

Educating yourself, working hard, and treating people well also worked for me, and applying these three success principles will work for you. No matter the barriers in your life, you can succeed in this great country.

Ricardo González is the founder and executive director of Bilingual America. He is an expert in the development of Spanish- and English-language courses and in helping companies and organizations to work effectively with Latinos. He also writes a popular blog about Hispanic/Anglo relations at www.gonzalezreport.com.

Principle 3:

Learn Every Day

*Learning is not attained by chance,
it must be sought for with ardor
and attended to with diligence.*

—ABIGAIL ADAMS,

wife of John Adams, the second president

of the United States

$\mathcal{W}$hen I was very young I was interested in everything. I wanted to know about caterpillars and butterflies and history stories and fireflies and birds and everything else. I was constantly asking, "What does this mean? What is that? Why are they different?" and a host of other questions. I was very lucky that my family encouraged me to learn constantly. My grandmother Ethel Daugherty had been a schoolteacher, and she taught me to read before I went to school. She said over and over, "You can learn anywhere, from anyone. Keep your eyes and ears open."

My own life experience has taught me that there are great opportunities to learn all around you if you are dedicated to being a willing and constant learner. If you are not learning every day, you are missing one of the great joys of life.

Newt

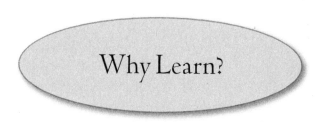

Why Learn?

It's what you learn after you know it all that counts.

—John Wooden

The world is larger than you. There are other towns, cities, countries, cultures, and languages outside of your own. There are as many different perspectives and thought processes as there are people. So while you might be familiar with your community, if you simply step outside its boundaries, you will be in a new environment. Some people react to the unknown with fear, because they do not know what to expect. Others react with excitement, because they suddenly have an opportunity to learn about new places, new people, and new cultures.

It's also true that once you understand a particular environment, you are not done learning. Over time, people and places change and evolve. The experience of driving into Atlanta in the 1970s is not the same experience as driving into Atlanta in 2009. Buildings have been demolished and new ones erected, people have moved in and out, and the culture of the city has transformed. Same name, same city, same geographic location, different experience.

No matter how much knowledge you absorb, you will always find people who know more. That's the exciting part—learning is a lifelong endeavor. Take advantage and learn from others. While you might know more math, they might know more science. While you might play football, they might play in a band. The way to learn every day is to fall in love with learning, to enjoy the process of acquiring and understanding new information. Everyone has something valuable to teach you if you are willing to listen and learn.

As you age, your goals will change. Because of this, the skills, habits, and knowledge you need to achieve them will change. The skills that helped you get through one area of life are only a building block for the next phase.

Learning and growing is the only way that you can develop into the person that you have the potential to become. If those around you try to tell you that it is not important to learn, don't listen to them. They mistakenly believe that they have learned everything and have nothing left to learn. They are wrong—there is always something to learn in some area of your life.

In your daily life, you will have many opportunities for learning if you allow yourself to slow down and pay attention. Take the time to stop, listen, and learn.

Mary Matalin, *political strategist, notes the impact of experiences on learning and education.*

~

The five principles of this wonderful book are timeless. But the Information Age promises to provide opportunities for today's young people beyond our imagining at this moment. Most exciting is that there will be absolutely no barriers to these opportunities for anyone anywhere except education. So, though getting a good education is always a top principle, it will be the threshold principle in the new age.

My definition of education includes adventures and experiences. I am encouraging my girls to travel and experience and do any number of off-the-beaten-path adventures to expand their educational reach. In the end, the only real success is to look back on a life richly lived, not one in pursuit of riches.

Mary Matalin's experience in politics, public affairs, crisis management, and media spans three decades and multiple venues. She began her involvement with politics at the grass-roots level in her native Illinois. The Reagan Revolution took her to Washington, where she served presidents Ronald Reagan, George H. W. Bush, and George W. Bush. Before joining the Bush/Cheney White House, Matalin hosted CNN's critically acclaimed debate show *Crossfire*.

Learning Anywhere, from Anyone

*A sense of curiosity is nature's original
school of education.*

—Smiley Blanton, psychiatrist

Americans love the idea of formal learning: we move from elementary school to middle school to high school to college and finally to graduate school. The curricula are set and the results are tracked and reviewed. There is great value in formal education, but learning entails much more than attending class and passing an exam: True learning is not so much about being in school or getting a degree, it's more about acquiring new, useful information and applying it to your life. It can be done anywhere, by anyone, and is an ongoing process.

Often we learn by applying information that we've picked up in one particular area to a new situation. Applying information to your life shows that you have firsthand knowledge of an area. Sharing that knowledge with others is what really brings it home to you, and often, the best way to know a subject is to teach it. Real learning comes with the application of knowledge in such a way that you make a difference in your life or in the lives of others.

If you are about to embark on a career in a new field, look toward others who have been successful in that field. Ask them to give you advice and pass along their knowledge to you. Many people will be glad to mentor you. If they say they are too busy, or do not want to help you, do not be discouraged, just turn your sights elsewhere until you find someone who is able and willing to help.

The more connectivity we have as a society through the Internet, and the more access to information, the more people will begin learning on an individual, ad hoc basis. You will be the one responsible for your learning and education.

Jackie's story about learning while on vacation illustrates the point of learning anywhere, from anyone:

During a recent Thanksgiving holiday, my family spent a week at my husband's grandmother's house on St. Simons Island off the coast of Georgia.

On Thanksgiving morning, my husband, my son, and I decided to brave the overcast weather and join a boat tour of the marsh surrounding the island. On the boat, a passenger asked the captain about the impact of the upcoming "flood tide," a term I had never heard before. My ears perked up—something new to learn about.

I learned that a flood tide occurs when the high tide is higher than normal, creating a flood in low-lying areas. This flooding allows redfish to swim into areas that are normally dry, providing them with access to fiddler crabs, which are normally not available to them. This opportunity for the redfish to feed ends up being an opportunity for anglers to catch a lot of fish in one place.

Flood tides occur once a month, with the full moon. If you know when they are going to occur, you can take advantage of the opportunity and, potentially, catch more fish than normal.

But for those who are not aware of the flood tide, one person's opportunity becomes another's hazard. During the flood tide, a boat can travel far into the marsh, and when the water recedes, the boat and its passengers can be left high and dry, stuck in an area that will not see tidewater again for another month.

Once this occurs, they are left with the option of dragging the boat through the mud, back into the water, or leaving it until the next flood tide dislodges it.

Serious fishing fans study the tides and phases of the moon to determine the best times to fish certain areas. They talk to other, more experienced fishers and watch the flood tides over time to see where the water will go. For them, knowledge is power, and learning is integral to their success. They know they can increase their chances of success by showing up at the right place, at the right time, with the right equipment (including, in this case, a jig—a fishing lure with a lead sinker, a hook, and a soft body covering made to resemble a fiddler crab). Rather than leave their fishing to chance, these people attempt to provide themselves with the best opportunity to succeed.

Thus, they are more likely to take advantage of the opportunity the flood tide provides. But an ill-prepared fisher can squander that same opportunity. This story reminds me that routinely followed paths are often not always the best to follow. We have to pay attention to *the current situation and make adjustments as necessary to reach our goal.*

Opportunities to learn will occur throughout life, at every turn. Sometimes, we are able to take advantage of them; other times we do not even recognize them.

You too have the ability to create new opportunities to learn. Join a civic organization, a church outreach group, or a running, biking, or swimming club. Meet new people, ask questions. Become interested in others and you will become interesting to them and learn along the way.

Questions you might ask yourself include: Are you paying attention to the surrounding landscape? Do you prepare for and then recognize opportunities so you can take advantage of them while they exist? When opportunities present themselves, do you have all the equipment necessary to take full advantage of them? Are you learning every day?

Political correspondent Tucker Carlson *talks about learning from anyone anywhere.*

~

The *Washington Post* used to conduct a writing drill in which reporters were assigned a name, picked at random from the phone book, and told to write a story about that person. I never read a boring one.

If you ask the right questions, everyone has something interesting to say—about four and a half hours' worth, to be precise. I've learned this in seventeen years of flying back and forth from Washington, D.C., to Los Angeles. Most people fear in-flight conversations with strangers. I ask a steady stream of questions, and have been rewarded with a graduate-level education in the human condition. I've learned all about what hundreds of people do for a living, how much they make, and why they get married, divorced, and drunk, not to mention what the Korean War was like and how a diesel engine works, among countless other things. I'm always smarter by the time I land.

Tucker Carlson is a political campaign correspondent for MSNBC. Until March 2008 he was the host of MSNBC's *Tucker,* a nightly news-and-opinion program.

Carlson joined MSNBC in February 2005 from CNN, where he was the youngest anchor in the history of that network. At CNN, he hosted a number of shows, including the network's political debate program *Crossfire.* During the same period, Carlson also hosted a weekly public affairs program on PBS.

A longtime magazine and newspaper journalist, Carlson has reported from around the world, most recently from Iraq and Lebanon. He has been a columnist for *New York* magazine and *Reader's Digest.* He currently writes for *Esquire,* the *New York Times Magazine,* and the *Daily Beast.* Carlson began his journalism career at the *Arkansas Democrat-Gazette* newspaper in Little Rock. His first book is entitled *Politicians, Partisans, and Parasites: My Adventures in Cable News.* In 2006 he competed on ABC's *Dancing with the Stars.* He is the host of the game show *Do You Trust Me?,* which is under development at CBS.

Tom Peters, *management guru and author of fifteen books, learns from everyone around him.*

~

L earning is not limited to book learning—it just starts there. The secret is learning from everyone, because everyone has a story to tell—if only you ask. And if only you listen—really listen.

In the United States, many of our newly arrived immigrants end up driving a cab for at least a while. I love to ride in cabs and get their stories. (They're so much more interesting, and trying, than mine!) Some foreign policy issue that concerns you? Wow, end up with a cabbie who came here from, say, Nigeria. Ask him about life there, his family here, his family members still back home. I guarantee you that in the space of a simple twenty-minute ride you'll learn more than you do from the *New York Times* and the *Washington Times* combined.

Tom Peters is coauthor of *In Search of Excellence*—a book voted by Bloomsbury Press as the best business book of all time, and with millions of copies in print. He has spoken on "people first" management more than 2,500 times in 63 countries since the book's publication in 1982. He is also the author of fifteen other business bestsellers.

 *U.S. Navy Admiral* Jim Stavridis, *commander of the U.S. Southern Command, understands the importance of learning every day.*

O ne of the most important things someone can do to become successful is to learn something new each and every day. Reading is the most obvious way to do that—so read and read and read.

But not everyone knows the value of questioning those around us with whom we come in contact. Every day I meet interesting men and women who are doing things completely different from what I do: chefs, bankers, electricians, photographers, politicians, security guards, airplane pilots, winemakers—the list goes on and on.

Admiral James Stavridis is a native of south Florida and a 1976 distinguished graduate of the U.S. Naval Academy. At the start of the Global War on Terror, he was selected as the director of the Navy Operations Group (Deep Blue). He has also served as the executive assistant to the secretary of the navy and the senior military assistant to the secretary of defense. He has served as a surface warfare officer, commanding the destroyer U.S.S. *Barry,* and as commander of the United States Southern Command.

Learning Requires Engagement

The important thing is to not stop questioning.

—Albert Einstein

To learn, you have to focus. Focus requires engaging in the activity or the thought process. Too often we think that being present is enough. It is not. You have to be more than present; you have to be engaged.

Engagement occurs when you focus all your attention on the activity at hand. Many psychologists believe that it is easiest to become engaged in learning when we are interested in a subject. This ties into why your big dream should be connected to your talent and interests. It is important to have a dream that excites you, in an area that you can learn about for the rest of your life. If you follow someone else's dream, it will be impossible to sustain the level of engagement needed for real learning and mastery for any length of time.

This need for engagement was recently highlighted on a tour Jackie took of the Ron Clark Academy—located in southeast Atlanta—in 2008, the high school's first year. Its namesake is the winner of the 2000 Disney Teacher of the Year Award and the lead figure in the 2006 TNT movie *The Ron Clark Story.*

This school was unlike any I had seen. The walls were bright colors, the second floor included a spiral slide that provided a quick way down to the lobby for students, teachers, and visitors alike.

The students were well behaved, looking me in the eye, shaking my hand, and introducing themselves. They responded to me with "Yes, ma'am" and "No, ma'am." The high level of discipline was part of what Clark terms the Essential 55, the essential rules for the classroom.

I went on the tour with several members of Leadership Atlanta, a group of business leaders trying to learn about new solutions in education and new principles of success.

Kim Bearndon, our tour guide and the cofounder of the academy, told us that the school's high level of discipline provides the framework for the creative and fun environment in the academy.

Touring the first floor, we could hear and feel a loud beat coming from above our heads. It was almost as if the ceiling was shaking. The first floor included a Delta classroom, named after the airline, complete with a ticket counter. It also contained a room labeled "The Gauntlet," where students take tests, many of which are hands-on activities.

At one end of the second-story hall was a library with a fireplace on the left-hand side, a couch on the right, and a bookcase along the back wall. In a building whose other rooms were filled with color and light, the library's dark colors appeared to be a throwback to an older time of gas lighting. But it was more than it appeared. Kim pressed a button on the side wall, the bookcase slid apart, and we entered Clark's classroom. The entrance was modeled after one of Clark's favorite childhood memories—the bookcase in the cartoon Scooby-Doo *opens that way.*

When we entered the classroom, the students and Clark were singing and stomping to a song about math, with Clark and many of the students standing on their desks. Once the song ended, the students rapidly sat in their seats and the class continued.

The math problem was about the cost of visiting Coney Island. This included riding the Ferris wheel and buying drinks and hot dogs (with and without cheese). Discounts were to be applied to all but the Ferris wheel. Once the problem was laid out on the board, each student began working independently to solve the problem.

Clark walked on the students' desks (yes, on the desks), checking work, praising those who had correctly solved the problem, and encouraging those who had the wrong answer to go back and try again.

After a few minutes, each student took a turn at the front of the class, attempting to solve the problem. Clark encouraged those who had not gotten the correct answer to share with the rest of the class where they had made their mistakes. Clark made it clear that he expected the students to pay attention and learn, and the students were clearly engaged.

At one point, one of the students went to the board and said an unacceptable phrase—apparently by accident. Clark's quick and low "Don't say that" was all the reproof required. The student checked himself and continued, but was obviously upset. After correctly finishing his portion of the problem, he sat down briefly, then got up and walked out of the classroom as the lesson continued. He returned a few minutes later.

The class moved to a different problem. With the students shouting out the answer to each step, Clark completed part of the problem. He then called for the student who had briefly left the classroom to return to the front to work the problem.

Prior to sitting down, Clark erased part of the problem and wrote in the wrong answer. When the student stood up, he noticed that the number was wrong. Clark acknowledged his mistake and told the student to correct it.

I am not sure, but my guess is that Clark's mistake was a deliberate one, intended to be part of the learning experience. It showed the student that even the teacher could make a mistake and that there was no shame involved in simply correcting it and moving on.

Clark's ability to incorporate this into the lesson, at the appropriate time—a teachable moment—provides a glimpse into what makes him a top teacher.

It's not the dancing on the desks or the chants and stomps; it's Clark's ability to connect with and engage *his students that makes him a master teacher. The sing-ing and stomping are his tools. Clark cares about his students, has high expectations for them, and teaches through real-life situations.*

I'm not suggesting all teachers should stand on desks. But tactics are important. It's about engaging students' attention, getting them interested in learning, and help-ing them improve themselves.

We probably all have memories of teachers who chal-lenged us and drove us to learn more.

Personal interaction and engagement are the require-ments for learning. Make sure you are not simply pres-ent, but engaged and ready to learn.

Admiral Ed Giambastiani Jr.

talks about moving beyond being a person who learns—by becoming a learning organization.

~

Newt's five principles are powerful keys to personal and professional success in life. In the military, however, personal success takes a backseat to *unit* or *team* success. Over my forty-one years in uniform, I've learned and taught the following four principles to help servicemen and -women develop personally in order for the team to be successful: competence, confidence, integrity, and stamina. Let me address just one here, competence. You have to master the details of your profession of arms. You have to become the expert at what you do and work hard to develop and expand your expertise. When you are new, your troops will know more than you, and that's by design. Don't be afraid to ask for help. Competence requires a questioning attitude. You must question assumptions, verify data, and seek multiple sources of information. It requires dedication

5 PRINCIPLES FOR A SUCCESSFUL LIFE

to continuous learning on both an individual and an organization level. My experience is that the best military units are the best not only because they have higher standards and they enforce them, but also because they turn themselves into "learning organizations."

Admiral Ed Giambastiani Jr. most recently served as the nation's seventh vice chairman of the Joint Chiefs of Staff. He currently serves as the chairman of Alenia North America Inc.

While on active duty, he held numerous positions, including command at the submarine, squadron, fleet, allied, and joint-service levels. He has extensive experience in nuclear-propulsion plant operations in addition to organizations responsible for experimentation and change. He has served as commander, United States Joint Forces Command, and as NATO's first supreme allied commander transformation (SACT).

Former lieutenant governor of Maryland, current RNC chairman, and chairman of GOPAC, Michael Steele *understands the importance of listening instead of talking.*

⁓

"Learning is a lifelong process," my mother used to say, "that begins the minute you shut up and listen." So I learned how to listen, and in the process, I learned how to apply the lessons of the classroom and the neighborhood to realize my dreams. It was not always easy or necessarily exciting, but it was important.

Now is your turn to listen and to learn the lessons that will help you realize the dreams that will define the twenty-first century. No matter how rocky or winding the road, the wonderful destination ahead of you will make the trip worthwhile—if you're willing to "shut up and listen."

Michael S. Steele earned his place in history in 2003 when he became the first African American elected to statewide office in Maryland. Steele is an expert on political strategy, fund-raising, PACs, and election reform. He is the current

Republican National Committee (RNC) chairman and chairman of GOPAC. He is also a partner in the international law firm of Dewey & LeBoeuf in Washington, D.C. Steele received a 2005 Bethune-DuBois Institute Award for his ongoing work in the development of quality education in Maryland and serves on a variety of boards and commissions.

Learning Through Failure

You have to be willing to learn new things every day,
every second. You can't depend on what you've
already been taught.

—Russell Simmons,
hip-hop musician and fashion mogul

Failure is not only an obstacle to be expected and overcome, it is also an opportunity to learn. How you perceive failure will determine how you react to failure when it happens.

Carol Dweck talks about the importance of our beliefs in her book *Mindset.* According to Dr. Dweck, the belief in our ability to affect our intelligence might be more important than our actual intelligence. Whether students believe in a growth mindset or a fixed mindset affects how hard they will work and how they will react to inevitable failure. Her research has indicated that it's better for children to believe that hard work matters than to believe that they are smart.

Students with a growth mindset believe that "intelligence is malleable and can be developed through education and hard work," she writes. The ones who hold a fixed mindset "believe that intelligence is a fixed trait."

Which group do you fit into?

"The students with a growth mindset felt that learning was a more important goal in school than getting good grades," she writes. "In addition, they held hard work in high regard, believing that the more you labored at something, the better you would become at it. They understood that even geniuses have to work hard for their great accomplishments."

When failure occurred, "students with a growth mindset said they would study harder or try a different strategy for mastering the material." Their belief that they had an impact on the outcome through the application of their effort led them to work harder or create a new approach.

"The students who held a fixed mindset, however, were concerned about looking smart with little regard for learning," she notes. "They had negative views of effort, believing that having to work hard at something was a sign of low ability. They thought that a person with talent or intelligence did not need to work hard to do well."

This also affected the response to roadblocks or out-and-out failures. "Attributing a bad grade to their own lack of ability, those with a fixed mindset said that they would study less in the future, try never to take that subject again, and consider cheating on future tests."

While this might appear counterintuitive on the surface, it makes perfect sense. Why would people apply effort if they believe that the outcome is predestined? If you were labeled smart or stupid forever, then effort would not matter.

This means that our steady stream of praise to our children for being "smart" has been undermining their potential performance. After all, if they really are so smart, there is more at risk if they fail and lose the label of being smart. If they are labeled unintelligent, then they will believe they cannot learn.

What if, instead of being labeled "smart" or "unintelligent," kids were told that brains grow and develop and that their ability to learn is linked to hard work and effort?

Students can control how hard they work and the effort they expend. They can learn to reevaluate a situation after failure to determine if more work or a different approach might lead to the desired results. They cannot control being labeled dumb or smart. The ability to have an impact on an outcome affects whether they think it is worth working for a different outcome.

The important lesson is not that people are smart or stupid but that through effort and hard work, brains can grow and people can change. In every event, you can ask yourself, "What can I learn from this experience?"

One of the best questions that you can ask is "How can I improve?" Whether you ask your customers, spouse, friends, or vendors, all of us can improve how we interact with others. This ability to question leads to learning and to improvement on a daily basis. If you want to learn, just ask the person next to you how you can improve.

Now that you have your big dream and are working

and learning from your mistakes, it's time to lighten up a bit and begin to enjoy life, with the understanding that the enjoyment of life is what keeps us going when we have to work hard and when we experience setbacks through interim failures.

Carly Fiorina—*business leader, bestseller, and speaker—notes the importance of learning.*

~

Both my parents pursued excellence in everything they did. Learning was not simply a way to make a living—learning was a goal in and of itself. My parents' expectations were passed to me and I soon found that whether it was through learning the piano as a child or moving from job to job as a young adult, learning something new could be a completely rewarding experience. My love of learning has continued throughout my life and career. If we have been in the same kind of job for too long, our perspective will inevitably narrow. All people and all organizations, regardless of their past successes, face a time when the current answers just aren't sufficient anymore—because the world around them has changed. Then, the only way to succeed is to take risks and try new things. Relying on old habits may be more comfortable, but creativity yields better results.

Carly Fiorina is a bestselling author, sought-after speaker, business commentator, and strategic adviser. As chairman and CEO of Carly Fiorina Enterprises, she is bringing her unique perspective and experience to bear on the challenging issues of our world, championing economic growth and empowerment for a more prosperous and secure world. In her memoir, *Tough Choices,* a *New York Times* and international bestseller that has been translated into twelve languages, Fiorina talks about her life and her views on leadership, technology, and workplace diversity.

Throughout an extraordinary career in business, she successfully blazed new trails and defied the odds. Fiorina was the first and, to date, only woman to lead a Fortune 20 company, and served as the chairman and CEO of Hewlett-Packard Company from 1999 to 2005. Most recently she served as victory chair for Senator John McCain's presidential bid, providing economic advice and public advocacy.

Tom Brokaw *explains how he has learned through failure and why it is an important opportunity.*

~

Never fail to learn from your failures, large and small. The most instructive experiences in my life have not been my successes; they've been my stumbles.

Why did I stumble? How can I avoid making the same mistake again? Be honest. Don't blame others when it was your fault you didn't succeed.

And when you do succeed, remember the failures so you don't begin to think the successes are part of your birthright.

Finally, be humble and gracious in victory—and resolute in defeat.

Tom Brokaw is one of the most trusted and respected figures in broadcast journalism. He began his career in 1962 at KMTV in Omaha, Nebraska. He anchored the late-evening news on Atlanta's WSB-TV in 1965 before joining KNBC-TV in Los Angeles. Brokaw was hired by NBC News in

1966, and from 1976 to 1981 he anchored NBC News's *Today* program.

On December 1, 2004, Brokaw stepped down after twenty-one years of serving as the anchor and managing editor of *NBC Nightly News.* Most recently, he served as interim moderator of NBC's *Meet the Press* and is currently a special correspondent for NBC News.

Along the way Brokaw has earned numerous lifetime achievement awards and broadcast journalism awards, as well as recognition for his devoted service to bringing exclusive interviews and stories to public attention.

The NBC News anchor also has a distinguished record as a political reporter, having interviewed every president since Lyndon B. Johnson and covered every election since 1968.

Complementing his distinguished broadcast journalism career, Brokaw has written essays and commentary for several publications, including the *New York Times,* the *Washington Post,* the *Los Angeles Times, Newsweek,* and *Time.* In addition, he became a bestselling author in 1998 with the publication of *The Greatest Generation* (Random House).

Principle 4:

Enjoy Life

Pleasure in the job puts perfection in the work.

—ARISTOTLE

$\mathcal{I}$n the hustle and bustle of daily life, many of us neglect our earliest passions in favor of pursuing unsatisfying work or short-term, empty goals like "making it to the weekend." We forget that it is entirely possible—and necessary for truly fulfilling work—to incorporate what we love into our daily routines.

For example, my early interest in animals and zoos led to my first experiences with public policy. I was ten years old, and after watching a matinee of two animal films in a theater in downtown Harrisburg, I noticed a sign that said "City Hall" and pointed through an alley. My grandmother had told me always to do my duty, and I decided my duty was to try to get a zoo for our city. I promptly walked over to ask how Harrisburg could get its own zoo. A kind park official (who, I learned later, had dated my grandmother forty years earlier) took the time to show me the records for the Harrisburg Zoo, which had existed in the 1930s. He explained that city officials had closed the zoo during World War II because of rationing, and he challenged me to personally convince city officials that Harrisburg needed a new zoo. He then called my grandmother and said he was sending me home in a cab, but I had to come back Tuesday to the city council meeting. The next Tuesday, I was right there waiting for the meeting, and the following day's edition of the *Harrisburg Patriot-News* featured a story on a certain ten-year-old boy championing the immediate construction of a local zoo. I was hooked on both zoos and citizenship from that point on.

Years later, while representing my Georgia district in Congress, I again had the opportunity to use my passion for zoos by contributing to my hometown Zoo Atlanta's fund-raising efforts. My passion—helping the zoo acquire exotic, beautiful animals like Boma, the black rhino; Yang Yang and Lun Lun, Chinese giant pandas; and even Komodo dragons—was part of my life as a citizen and as a public official.

I've always thoroughly enjoyed using my work to help protect animals and the environment—not only because I am personally intrigued by the incredible diversity found in nature but also because I believe that we are called upon to be stewards of the natural world. We have an obligation to preserve and protect it for future generations of all kinds of animals, which is why I played a key role in saving the Endangered Species Act during the late 1990s, and why, more recently, I wrote *A Contract with the Earth* with Terry L. Maple, director of the Palm Beach Zoo. In the book, we call for a bipartisan approach to environmentalism, so that all Americans can work to protect the fragile species diversity on our planet.

These are just a few examples of how and why I have tried to help animals thrive in their natural habitat, where they are protected from outside threats. I have been blessed with a career that has allowed me to focus my energy on the things that are most important to me. Yet it is always important to remember that, regardless of your particular job or background, you must use your own talents and strengths to make a difference in the lives of others. After focusing on citizenship for forty-plus years, I am convinced that helping those around us is vital for truly enjoying life; a selfish existence is an empty one, and when we are using whatever means we have to do the most good we can, then we are really living.

Newt

Why Enjoy Life?

Happiness depends upon ourselves.

—Aristotle

Today is the day God has given you. There will be many things to enjoy about today if you relax and let yourself take pleasure in them. Most of these things will be free. The sunrise will be beautiful. The birds' songs will enchant you. Each food will have a unique taste. A glass of water after exercise will be delightful.

How many things can you savor and enjoy out of a day?

Will you let yourself enjoy them?

If you are going to pursue a big dream, you already know you are going to have to work hard. But to be able to work hard enough to achieve your big dream, you have to be able to really enjoy the journey you're on. We've found there are two ways to create this fulfill-ment and pleasure. First, you have to develop habits and patterns that allow you to be gratified by your work every day. Learn to look forward to certain tasks in your work. It is important to create a work life that brings you pleasure during the workday, not something that's just a means to an end. Second, you have to learn how to take regular breaks from the business of everyday life. You need a time to recharge, whether it's reading for fif-teen minutes at the end of the day or shutting off your BlackBerry for a real vacation. These breaks will revive you so you can go on to conquer the next wave of work your big dream requires.

There should be aspects of your work and learning that are truly gratifying to you. This is not to suggest every step of your journey has to be fun. You may have a dream so important to you that you are willing to do a lot of things you do not enjoy to accomplish it. But the faster you can teach yourself to appreciate each task on your path and to find satisfaction in its achievement, the more likely you are to achieve your dream.

Gratification evokes feelings of pleasure and joy from within. It is not derived from bodily pleasure but is about employing personal strengths and virtues. Being totally engaged in playing in a professional football game is probably not "pleasurable," but when a player is able to use his athletic skills successfully, he's pleased with his performance.

As your skills develop in an area, and as you push yourself to reach new goals, gratification comes when you are able to meet a challenge by stretching those skills. Sometimes the greatest sense of accomplishment comes when we achieve something we thought was just outside our grasp.

In the spring of 2008, Jackie was a guest on the live Canadian Business News Network program *Squeeze Play*. Because she was being questioned while in Atlanta, she couldn't see the hosts. It was the first time she'd been the person answering tough questions on live television, and her earpiece and microphone were her only connection to the rest of the program. It was a new challenge.

I was a bit nervous, but a few deep breaths helped calm me down. When the show started, there was feedback in my earpiece, so when I talked there was an echo of my voice in my ear. Instead of panicking, I simply ignored the feedback and was able to complete the interview and get the important points across. Clearly this was new and outside my experience, but I was able to perform under pressure, and this definitely provided a great sense of accomplishment and satisfaction.

Pleasure, on the other hand, contains strong emotional elements. For you, that may mean purchasing a new outfit or electronic gadget or eating a good meal. These activities should be enjoyed as respites from hard work—not as the main goal but as a diversion. Movies are a great way to get away from work at hand. In the 1970s, our family often drove in from Carrollton, Georgia, to Atlanta, which was about an hour away. We would spend the day at the movies, watching two or three movies in a stretch. We acknowledge that not everyone would find that pleasurable, but we sure did!

Research by Barbara Fredrickson at the University of North Carolina at Chapel Hill found that positive emotions such as joy and contentment have "the potential to broaden people's habitual modes of thinking and build their physical, intellectual, and social resources." Negative emotions—fear, anxiety, stress—tend to narrow thought and action tendencies. In other words, it is harder for people to think of potential options when they are experiencing negative emotions than when they are experiencing positive emotions.

Seek pleasures that allow you to escape the bustle of everyday activity and relax. Create patterns of activities that help you experience gratification, joy, and contentment, thereby making the process of working hard enjoyable throughout your life.

Rush Limbaugh, *nationally syndicated radio host, notes the importance of enjoying life.*

~

It is said that without struggle, there is no purpose. I believe that. But struggle need not be suffering. We only get one life, and I have come to believe that God intended for each of us to get the *most* out of it we can, including enjoying and loving it, accompanied by constant thanks and appreciation of it. There will, of course, be suffering, but the self-induced variety, usually brought on by pessimistic predictions of a future we cannot possibly know, is needless and destructive. There should be *no* guilt in the pursuit of happiness and the enjoyment of life.

Rush Limbaugh launched his phenomenally successful radio broadcast into national syndication on August 1, 1988, with fifty-six radio stations. Twenty years later it is heard on nearly six hundred stations by approximately twenty million people each week and is the highest-rated national radio talk show in America.

In addition to his radio program, broadcast weekdays from noon to three P.M. ET, Limbaugh hosts *The Rush Limbaugh Morning Update*, a ninety-second commentary that debuted in March 1992 and airs Monday through Friday. *The Rush Limbaugh Show* and *The Rush Limbaugh Morning Update* are produced and distributed by Premiere Radio Networks.

Recognized for his achievements, Limbaugh received the Marconi Award for Syndicated Radio Personality of the Year, given by the National Association of Broadcasters, in 1992, 1995, 2000, and 2005. In 1993, he was inducted into the Radio Hall of Fame, and in 1998, into the National Association of Broadcasters Hall of Fame.

Being Grateful and Pleasant

Every dog has his day, but it's not every dog that knows when he's having it.

—Winifred Gordon, artist

One of the best ways to enjoy life is to be grateful. Being grateful means being thankful for what you have and for whom you are with. It allows you to enjoy what is already around you: the beautiful weather, the food you eat, the people you meet, the ability to wash your clothes in a washing machine. To be grateful, all you have to do is slow down and look around at what you have—while not comparing yourself with anyone else.

To express gratitude, you must acknowledge that you are better off because of forces outside your control and be thankful to the benefactor that has provided this benefit. Expressing gratitude is the opposite of complaining. As the Greek philosopher Epictetus said, "He is a man of sense who does not grieve for what he has not, but rejoices in what he has."

Before you can express gratitude, you have to be aware of what you have. Often we overlook items for which we should be grateful—we take them for granted or believe we are entitled to them. A simple shift in your mindset can make a profound difference in how you view your life, which can then change your thinking.

Researchers Robert Emmons from the University of California, Davis, and Michael McCullough from the University of Miami have addressed the influence of grateful thinking in their paper "Counting Blessings Versus Burdens."

Findings from two of the studies discussed in the paper really interested us. In the first study, three groups were created. One was asked to count blessings, another hassles, and the third events. There were 192 participants who completed ten weekly reports. Those who counted blessings rated their lives more favorably, exercised more (almost 1.5 hours more per week), and rated their health better than did those in the other two groups.

In the second study, the three groups were separated

into those who kept track of their gratitude, hassles, and downward social comparison (compared with those who were not as well off socially). For sixteen days, each of the 157 participants completed a worksheet. Those in the gratitude group reported they were more "attentive, determined, energetic, enthusiastic, excited, interested, joyful, strong," than did those in the other two groups. They also reported to be more likely to have helped others.

In these studies, the participants' lives didn't change. Instead, the way they reflected on and thought about their lives changed. Those who reflected on and recorded their blessings had a more positive outlook on their lives and thought of their lives as better than those who did not.

The takeaway? If you want a better life, begin by being grateful for the life you currently have. Become aware of the many blessings around you. One of the best and easiest ways to accomplish this is to spend five minutes a night reflecting on your day, and then writing down three things you are grateful for, being as specific as possible.

White Christmas, the 1954 classic holiday movie with music and lyrics by Irving Berlin, has a scene where Bob Wallace (Bing Crosby) and Betty Haynes (Rosemary Clooney), neither of whom can sleep, meet at the inn for a midnight snack. The scene results in the two of

them singing "Count Your Blessings (Instead of Sheep)."
The chorus of this song is:

> *When you're worried and you can't sleep*
> *Just count your blessings instead of sheep*
> *And you'll fall asleep counting your blessings*

So true. Our minds can hold only one thought at a time, so if we are busy counting our blessings, we cannot be fearful and scared and are instead relaxed and content.

With gratitude comes a sense of pleasantness. Few people want to spend time with someone who is not pleasant to be around. Try to be pleasant when you feel satisfied and, more important, when you are faced with obstacles. While it is extremely hard to be pleasant during times of stress and turmoil, these are often the times when doing so will provide the biggest payback.

Life unfolds moment by moment, day by day. It is important that we try to create a pleasant environment in which to live. Jackie's story reinforces the importance of doing just that:

> *We all have morning routines. At our house, the morn-*
> *ing routine includes an alarm clock, coffee, grits, eggs,*
> *brushing teeth, getting dressed, checking homework, and*
> *driving the children to school.*

The routine allows us to move through the mundane without thinking and gets us where we need to be (school, work) at the proper time. We all know exactly when we have to leave the house to make the car pool line on time, and most mornings we make it.

One morning a few years ago, while waiting at school in the car pool line to drop off my son Robert (who was then four years old), he and I had a few minutes to talk about the day ahead, what he would be doing, and when we would see each other next. As I always did before he trundled off to his preschool class, I finished the conversation with my reminder: "Every day, I love you."

This always brought a smile to his face (which I loved). Every day I gave him a quick kiss before he left the car. Some days, he walked straight into the school, while other days, he turned back for one last wave and assurance of my love.

I liked to think that that ritual helped him start his day properly, secure in the knowledge that he is loved and will return to the same safe place soon. That same year, Robert told me that "all the teachers say 'Hello' and 'Good morning!' to me as I walk through my school"; I could visualize him walking through the halls, responding in kind to those who gave him a word of welcome.

What a lovely feeling, that as you arrive somewhere, people are glad that you are there and are glad to see you. My happy boy, just assured by his mother of her love, walked through his school welcomed by all.

To feel totally welcomed is an incredible feeling. It releases tension from the body and makes you glad that you are there. It creates the right tone to start the day, leaving you relaxed and ready to focus on the work at hand.

Contrast this with the welcome that many of us adults receive when we go places. Often, the people with whom we come in contact are hurried and harried, there is little time for pleasantries, and we do not feel welcome. I have to admit that I am not as good about properly welcoming people as I would like to be. Often, I am more preoccupied with where I am going than with welcoming the people I see. For, in reality, aren't we all just grown-up children who would like to be welcomed wherever we go?

Make a point to be pleasant and welcoming to everyone with whom you come in contact. It will make your life, and their lives, richer and more pleasant. In addition, it will weave together a rich fabric of life that will be able to withstand the times of trouble that are sure to come to everyone's life.

General John P. Abizaid *(Retired), former Central Command commander, provides us with a view into why respect is important.*

~

I was raised in a poor but proud family from a small mountain town in California. Being true to my upbringing, I always tried to give the lowest-ranking soldier or the humblest villager the same respect that I gave the greatest leaders. Difficult service in difficult places taught me that respect is contagious.

John Abizaid served the United States for thirty-four years in combat zones in Grenada, Lebanon, Kurdistan, Bosnia, Kosovo, Afghanistan, and Iraq. His distinguished military service propelled him to become the commander of United States Central Command from 2003 to 2007.

Recovery

Courage consists in the power of self-recovery.

—Ralph Waldo Emerson

There is a rhythm of work and rest that is central to our ability to function well. No one can sustain unending effort without breaking down. There have to be periods of renewal to offset periods of all-out effort. Establishing the right rhythm for you will dramatically increase your ability to be effective and to achieve a lot.

There are four types of recovery: physical, emotional, mental, and spiritual. Physical recovery includes sleep, food, water, and exercise. Making sure that you have enough physical energy to be effective is key. Regular sleep patterns, good nutrition, staying hydrated, and physical activity provide a physical foundation that enables you to live your best life. General George Patton Jr. said, "Fatigue makes cowards of us all." The world often does appear better once you have had a good night's sleep. Afternoon naps, for as little as fifteen minutes, can serve as a welcome respite and provide you with enough energy to tackle the rest of your day. While these physical requirements might appear to be mundane, meeting them is an investment of time rather than an expenditure of time.

Emotional recovery is the relief from emotional distress, including fear, hopelessness, doubt, and anger. We all know what it is like to feel angry or hopeless. On occasion we can become overwhelmed with these emotions.

Negative emotions tend to stimulate our urge for immediate action, UNC researcher Barbara Fredrickson thinks, because it was immediate action that helped our ancestors survive threats to their lives. Positive emotions are thought to produce the opposite reaction. Instead of provoking immediate and fast responses, positive emotions, according to Fredrickson, broaden our ability to think, helping to build bonds and resources to be used later—when negative emotions reappear.

This "broaden and build" view of positive emotions provides a framework in which positive emotions become the cement and framework of the complex structure that is life. As we interweave our life with many friends, organizations, areas of interest, and communities, we build on and strengthen its structure. This complex structure later allows us to survive fast changes of pace when necessary.

When emotions run high, it is often helpful to step back, take a breath, and make sure that there are physical reasons for the high emotional response. Jackie, for example, gets hungry rapidly and knows that if her blood sugar gets too low she will become unpleasant to be around. She plans for several snacks during the day to ward off this potential trigger.

Mental recovery provides your brain with a rest. While hard work may get us ahead, it has limits. It's often the times of rest and recovery that provide us with the energy we need to work hard. In today's ultraconnected world of BlackBerrys, iPhones, e-mail, and Twitter, it is often hard to get even a few moments to yourself. Without the minibreaks that were once common in daily life, our brains have become switched to a constant "go" state, provoked by ceaseless stimuli.

Indeed, we often go in several directions at once, multitasking in an effort to get items off our "to-do" lists and onto our "done" lists. It's not unusual to see a driver also talking on the phone and even e-mailing—trying to get it all done.

There is a simple way to counteract this constant state of *on*—by turning *off* the mind a few minutes each day. Though this may seem simple to accomplish, it is not. The good news is that, according to *Train Your Mind, Change Your Brain,* by Sharon Begley, your brain can not only learn new material but can be taught new ways to process that material through meditation. This means that we can train our brains and thereby affect our emotions.

According to Begley, mental training through meditation focusing on love and compassion increases our feelings of happiness and contentment. Rather than reacting constantly to what happens to us based on our outer environment, we can literally rewire our brains by meditating, attaining the ability to summon calming, happy thoughts, and remaining in control. This takes only a few minutes, but the impact can be enormous. The ability to summon happy thoughts is critical when there is little time to recover and performance matters. Jackie tells the story of how her dad's ability to recover quickly helps him achieve peak performance:

Dad has always had the ability to close his eyes and take a few minutes' rest, no matter where he is. This ability to rest on the go has enabled him to maintain a pace that often wears out younger colleagues after a few weeks. A few years ago, he showed that he also has the ability to center himself rapidly and overcome obstacles.

He had a new book out, Winning the Future, *and was in Atlanta for promotional events. The schedule was packed with book signings and media appearances. Travel time was not downtime, but time to be used to call radio stations. I was traveling with him and knew there was not a minute of rest scheduled in the day. When we arrived at a TV studio in the morning to shoot multiple TV appearances via satellite, there was no one there for makeup.*

With less than ten minutes before his first appearance, I volunteered to do his makeup—which in this instance amounted to no more than simply brushing powder on his face to remove the shine. But I had forgotten to shake the brush, and a large amount of powder drifted down and settled on the top of the shoulder of his suit. We now had less than five minutes before air. Quick to assure him that this was not a disaster, I rushed to say, "Don't worry, it's okay as long as you don't—" And right at that second, he brushed the powder as I finished the sentence: "touch it." He gave me that "I'm not too amused" look. I just smiled, blew and brushed off the powder, and finished up. With a little over a minute to go, I said, "Close your eyes and go to your happy place." Well, I had never tried this before with him, but thought it could not hurt. It worked perfectly! Dad closed his eyes, took a few deep breaths, totally relaxed, and was fabulous when he went on air, on his game and looking perfect.

Spiritual recovery, whether through prayer, meditation, or service to others, provides us with the opportunity to rejuvenate our spirit. These activities are important, as they allow us to ground our spirit, reminding us who we really are inside.

Recovery is key to peak performance. Never taking a break will make you snap, but stretching and then recovering will help you grow. Challenge yourself by seeking out situations of stress, but be sure that you rest and recover afterward. The goal is to become stronger in all areas of your life without breaking or snapping. When you feel yourself get close to the edge, simply back off for a few minutes and then try again.

Throughout your life, make sure that you have time to relax and recover, to think good thoughts, and get ready for the work ahead.

Former president Bill Clinton *notes the importance of gratitude in helping him achieve his goals.*

I was born into a family without wealth or powerful connections. But from my mother and other relatives, I was given a more powerful gift: the belief that I could do anything I wanted in life with big dreams, hard work, and a genuine interest in and respect for other people. I was also taught that every day is a gift, that I should enjoy life, learn as much as I could in school, and be grateful for every good thing that happens.

Those lessons enabled me to live the American dream.

I hope you will set high goals, work hard to reach them, and enjoy your friends and your life. You can do great things.

William Jefferson Clinton was elected Arkansas attorney general in 1976 and won the governorship in 1978. After losing a bid for a second term, he regained the office four years later and served until his 1992 bid for the presidency of the United States. Elected president in 1992 and again in 1996, Clinton was the first Democratic president to win a second term in six decades. Under his leadership, the United States enjoyed the strongest economy in a generation and the longest economic expansion in U.S. history.

After leaving the White House, he established the William J. Clinton Foundation with the mission to strengthen the capacity of people in the United States and throughout the world to meet the challenges of global interdependence. Clinton has also developed the Clinton Foundation HIV/AIDS Initiative, the Clinton Global Initiative, and the Clinton Hunter Development Initiative and works closely with the American Heart Association on the Alliance for a Healthier Generation.

Giving to Others

Happiness . . . consists in giving and in serving others.

—Henry Drummond,
Scottish evangelist, 1851–1897

True charity comes from the heart as well as the mind. It reflects a shared sense of humanness. When you help someone, you increase your own sense of being human. When you help others, someday they may help you or one of your loved ones.

Giving is actually the most powerful form of receiving a gift. The recipient's happiness and gratitude reflect onto you and deepen your own joy.

The purpose of the book *Who Really Cares: The Surprising Truth About Compassionate Conservatism* is to "make the point that charity matters," according to author Arthur Brooks. He notes that charity is vital to our personal prosperity, happiness, and health and to the ability to express ourselves in a humane way.

"Charitable acts, such as giving and volunteering, tend to strengthen social networks between people," according to Brooks. "These networks stimulate economic success." Working with others to help others is in large part the purpose of community.

Charitable giving moves the focus from ourselves to others. It's not just the amount of money that we can give; it's also the ability to care and focus on someone else. Brooks cites a study conducted by researchers at Harvard Medical School "in which a group of 132 multiple sclerosis patients was split into two equal groups; one group was assigned to act charitably toward members of the other. The researchers found that the givers experienced a 'dramatic change in their lives,' in confidence, self-awareness, and depression; they enjoyed between three and seven times more improvement than the receivers of help."

So not only does charity assist those in need, it benefits those who give. Giving to others reminds you of the blessings that you have and also allows you to participate in improving someone's life.

Through the Learning Makes a Difference Foundation (LMDF), Jackie has been implementing one of her father's many ideas, paying middle school and high school students to learn math and science. Focusing on innovative learning programs, the foundation's Learn and Earn Pilot Program, with forty students, resulted in better academic scores in the Learn and Earn group than in the control group. Jackie talks about the results that affected her most:

> *It was thrilling to watch students who were initially unengaged and uninterested in math and science discover the thrill of learning. They finally understood that they can learn and that studying pays off. Halfway through the fifteen-week program, when one of the students turned to me with a big grin on his face and said, "I was failing," I smiled at his use of the past tense. He would pass the class. Changing people's lives for the better—that's what the Learning Makes a Difference Foundation is all about.*
>
> *These students inspired us to write the first draft of this book, and without them, I am not sure we would have finished it. Our goal was to hand a draft to them at the end of their program—and Dad and I reached our goal.*

"Studies have found that the more one volunteers, the greater the benefits," according to Brooks. This reflects the fact that charity is not just about money, but also about interest, time, and connection. My friends who have worked at nonprofits tell me they love to receive money, but are equally thrilled to receive time and talent. The latter gifts allow them to serve more of their target population.

The good news is that charitable giving appears to pay back, according to Brooks: "Two people who are identical with respect to age, religion, politics, sex, and race. The only difference is one gives money and volunteers his time annually, but the other does neither. . . . The charitable person will earn, on average, about $14,000 more per year than the uncharitable person."

Brooks determines that health, happiness, and income are part of a reinforcing cycle that includes giving and helping. Prosperous people are more likely to be charitable, and charitable people are more likely to be prosperous.

He expands on the theme of giving and happiness in *Gross National Happiness: Why Happiness Matters for America—and How We Can Get More of It*, noting that giving provides us with a sense of control. This sense of control provides us with a feeling of mastery in our life, which makes us happy. Focusing on problems of others crowds out our focus on and concern with our own problems. Giving produces a feeling of euphoria termed "helpers' high." This is due to the release of endorphins, the natural opiates in the brain.

Jackie talks about one of her first memories of working to make the world a better place:

> In the early 1970s, there was a Keep America Beautiful TV commercial advertisement that featured a Native American. Dressed in buckskin and feathers, surrounded by pollution, his simple statement was memorable: "People start pollution. People can stop it." As he spoke a tear rolled down his cheek. Every time I saw the ad, I wanted to cry too—it was clearly an effective advertisement. This was also the time of the Pitch-In campaign, reminding people to pitch in and throw away trash. At that time my father was a professor of environmental studies at the University of West Georgia in Carrollton, and our family often went with his students on field trips to the Okefenokee Swamp and the Flint River. I grew to love and appreciate the

outdoors. I also learned to "pitch in" and do my part at an early age.

In 1971, as part of the second Earth Day, we walked along the roads in Carrollton and picked up trash from the sides of the highway. As the trash bags became full, we would tie them and leave them for a truck to pick up later in the day. I was four years old at the time, and what I remember most is finding a toilet seat on the side of the road. I have no idea how it got there, but when we were done, it was gone.

This love for the land has shaped our interest and involvement in nonprofits. We have both been involved in the Trust for Public Land, a nonprofit group that saves land for people. Newt assisted in securing federal funding to save land along the Chattahoochee River, which provides water for Atlanta. Jackie serves on the advisory council of the Georgia chapter of the Trust for Public Land, so that children, including her own, can continue to enjoy the wilderness.

Give your time and talents in the service of others. You won't regret it.

Jim Clifton, *chairman and chief executive officer of Gallup Inc., talks about the benefits he received from developing others.*

~

I n high school and college I dreamed about doing something of global, colossal significance, never about being rich. Doing something socially important was my big dream. But at that age I didn't know what that might be. During college I worked at a youth prison, tutored Mexican Americans through their high school degrees, and was very active in the YMCA as a coach and camp wrangler. I mention these activities because they required hard work and took up a lot of time. But when I look back on the most hardworking and rewarding developmental times of my life, the events that changed me the most, it was not time I spent with college professors or on student activities but rather the time I spent developing someone else.

Jim Clifton is best known in the polling and survey research field for leading the acquisition of the Gallup Organization, founded by the renowned polling pioneer George H. Gallup. Under Clifton's leadership, Gallup has expanded from a predominantly U.S.-based company to a global organization with more than forty offices in twenty countries. The business world recognizes Clifton as the creator of the Gallup Path, a metric-based economic model that establishes the linkages among human nature in the workplace, customer engagement, and business outcomes.

His most recent innovation, the Gallup World Poll, is designed to give the world's six billion citizens a voice in key global issues. Clifton also serves on several boards and is chairman of the Thurgood Marshall Scholarship Fund.

Former lieutenant colonel
Oliver North *notes the*
importance of helping others to
fully enjoy life.

~

U se your God-given gifts and talents to honor Him, and you will be blessed. Know your own strengths and weaknesses, and that which you can do well will be obvious. Learn all you can about your chosen endeavor— even from your own mistakes. Do what you love, and hard work will never seem too hard. Surround yourself with those who hold you accountable, encourage you in failure, and admonish you to humility—and thank them for doing so. Never play "shoulda, woulda, coulda," and don't let a day pass without asking someone, "How can I help you?"

Former lieutenant colonel *Oliver L. North* is a combat decorated marine, a former U.S. Counter-Terrorism Coordinator, a number one bestselling author, an inventor with three U.S. patents, a syndicated columnist, and the host of *War Stories* on the Fox News Channel. Yet he says his most important accomplishment is being "the husband of one, the father of four, and the grandfather of eleven."

Born in San Antonio, Texas, North graduated from the U.S. Naval Academy in Annapolis, Maryland, and served twenty-two years as a U.S. Marine. His awards for service in combat include the Silver Star, the Bronze Star for Valor, and two Purple Hearts for wounds in combat.

Flowing Through Life

When I come into a game in the bottom of the ninth,
bases loaded, no one out, and a one-run lead . . .
it takes people off my mind.

—Tug McGraw,
major-league baseball relief pitcher

If your goal is not only to enjoy the pleasure of life but also to experience gratification, then you have to take control and create the experiences of flow.

Flow is the sense of effortless action, when everything seems to click perfectly into place. These are often the moments that stand out as being among the best in your life. Athletes often refer to being "in the zone," religious mystics call it the state of ecstasy, and artists call it rapture. If life is experience, and flow represents the best moments in our lives, it follows that you would want to create more flow, thereby increasing your best moments.

Time seems not to exist when you are so engrossed in an activity that you forget your worries, your fears, your unfinished errands. For those of us with to-do lists longer than a four-year-old's Christmas list, such interludes are rare moments of nirvana on Earth. It's at those moments that we feel we are really living life to the fullest. "To live means to experience—through doing, feeling, thinking," according to Mihaly Csikszentmihalyi, author of *Finding Flow,* who is best known for contributing the concept of flow to psychology.

But how do we find our flow? How can we create the moments where everything comes together as if without effort? How can we make all the pieces fit together, almost as if they are being drawn together by an unseen hand?

In *Authentic Happiness,* Martin Seligman asks, "When does time stop for you? When do you want to find yourself doing exactly what you want to be doing, and never wanting it to end?" Such moments, according to Seligman, occur when you are in a state of flow.

Think back over the past week and consider when

you were so totally absorbed in what you were doing that time appeared to stand still. For both of us, that often happens while reading or writing.

Flow is notable not just for the happiness that you experience during the event but also for the reflection and satisfaction you feel afterward, the ability to look back and say, "That was enjoyable," whether it was closing a contested business deal, winning a tennis match, or rearranging a closet.

The key components of flow include a task that is challenging and requires skill (is attainable but requires stretching and using all of one's strengths), concentration, clear goals, immediate feedback, effortless involvement, and a sense of control. When all this happens at the same time, the sense of self vanishes and time seems to be suspended. Rather than being separate from everything and everyone else, you are involved, and are able to flow through life.

You can create the structure necessary for flow in work and physical activities by setting continually higher goals, delegating items that are outside your area of expertise, and receiving feedback. The rest of life, however, is messier. Someone has to do the dishes, pay the bills, and pick up the dry cleaning.

We acknowledge you may not always find your flow while doing those tasks. But, according to Csikszentmihalyi, when one takes the whole context of the activity into account and understands the impact of one's action on the whole, a trivial job can become a memorable performance that leaves the world a more positive place than it was before. For these everyday tasks, a few tactics can increase the probability of attaining flow. They include placing the activity in the context of a larger goal, creating periodic goals, and exercising control over when and how the task is to be completed.

Jackie talks about ways to put this into practice:

While doing laundry is still not my favorite activity, it becomes a more pleasant task when I picture my children wearing the clothes I'm washing. Creating interim goals can help. For example, I may try to clean the house or sweep the porch at a faster pace, or I may attempt to find a way to improve the process of bill paying. Anything that removes my focus from the drudgery associated with the task itself is helpful.

A friend recently told me that she irons while watching Oprah. This allows her to enjoy watching the show while accomplishing a required but not well-loved task. Other people say they combine two disliked tasks to complete them in half the time it would take to do them separately—for instance, expense reports and waiting for airplanes.

While trying to reframe daily tasks so they become flow events is helpful, higher-level flow attainment requires effort, skill, and accepting the risk of failure. This is the flow that you feel when closing a deal, hitting a home run, or finishing a complex home project.

You can reach your goals by learning skills, putting those skills into action, and refusing to be immobilized by the fear of failure. If the goal is truly a big one, then the only way to accomplish it is by giving it your complete focus.

That will not only help you achieve your goals but will also help you enjoy the effort itself.

Now that you have a big dream and you are working hard, learning, and enjoying life, it's time for the next step: being true to yourself.

Award-winning actress Whoopi Goldberg *notes that being true to yourself throughout life is the key to success.*

~

I live by "Be true to yourself" because who else can you really be true to? Each decision you make moves you a little further in life. Sometimes, if you are true to other people's principles, they move you back. And if you adhere to someone else's principles, you may move forward, but somehow you're not as steady, you're not as clear, you're not as strong. True, it might be pleasing to other folks, but you may find yourself grumbling or, worse, doing things that don't feel quite right. It can be a very lonely road if your beliefs have you standing alone. It's easier to give in, but I find I'm never more myself than when I'm standing exactly where I should be: being the person I know I am. Like Shakespeare wrote: "To thine own self be true."

Whoopi Goldberg is one of an elite group of artists who have won Grammy, Academy, Golden Globe, Emmy, and Tony awards. She is equally well known for her humanitarian efforts on behalf of children, the homeless, human rights, education, and the battles against substance abuse and AIDS, as well as many other causes and charities. Among Goldberg's charitable activities is her service as a goodwill ambassador to the United Nations. She has been honored with multiple NAACP Image Awards, numerous People's Choice Awards (including a special tribute in 1998), and five Nickelodeon Kids' Choice Awards for Favorite Movie Actress, as well as various awards and honors for her many humanitarian efforts.

Goldberg currently appears as a moderator on ABC's long-running talk show *The View.*

Principle 5:

Be True to Yourself

Above all things,
to thine own self be true.

—WILLIAM SHAKESPEARE

$\mathcal{W}$hen I left the speakership in 1999, I found myself at an important turning point in my life. For the last twenty-six years, I had spent my time running for public office and serving as a member of Congress. All of a sudden, I was faced with the daunting challenge of thinking through a new career.

I had to stop and ask myself: *What do I really like doing? What do I truly value? How can I live up to my potential and be the best possible version of "me"?*

The more I thought about it, the more I realized what was important to me: I loved learning, I loved public service, and I cherished my independence.

Identifying these core values helped me to define what I would *not* do in the next stage of my career. I would not lobby because it would undermine my ability to speak out as an advocate for the public good. I would not take a job with one company or one firm because then that organization would own my time, and I would be forced to focus on *their* goals and *their* expectations, which would hinder my nature as an independent thinker.

In order to stay true to my values, I ultimately decided to develop a career in which I maintained control over my own schedule so that I could focus time on the important things—my family, enjoying life, and pursuing ideas that intrigued me.

The first step I took in the journey toward the next phase of my career was to set out and fulfill my never-ending passion for learning. I enthusiastically began to study science and technology and catch up on all of the new and amazing breakthroughs that had occurred while I was in office. Georgia Tech, NASA Ames, the National Science Foundation, and the American Museum of Natural History—all of these wonderful institutions opened up their vast resources to me and helped contribute to a new and exciting part of my ongoing education.

Once I armed myself with the tools, methods, and resources needed to accomplish the task at hand, I gathered together a group of impressive individuals who had been with me for years while I was in office. They became my core team, and we set out to establish a communications company and a consulting firm. The latter has now evolved into the Center for Health Transformation, an organization that has come to be recognized and respected nationally. As our goals and aspirations continued to grow, we added a productions company to create movies and produce audio books. The American Enterprise Institute also hosted me as a senior scholar on a part-time basis, and the Department of Defense offered me an opportunity to assist with national security through the Defense Policy Board and other activities. Each of these ventures has offered me the chance to nurture my entrepreneurial spirit and continue to serve the public in a meaningful way.

The last decade has been more energetic, challenging, tiring, and fulfilling than I ever could have imagined. I have had the privilege and opportunity to work with wonderful and talented people through exciting challenges that involve constant learning and a deep sense of public purpose. Being true to myself was the right decision.

Had I decided ten years ago to ignore my true values and passions and substitute them with a high-paying-yet-unsatisfying job, I know I would feel a significant sense of regret today.

By being true to myself I am living a much more enriched and colorful life, one that continues to inspire me and make me truly happy every day.

Next

Why Be True to Yourself?

*A man cannot be comfortable without
his own approval.*

—Mark Twain

Being true to yourself might sound easy, but it is not. It requires knowing who you are and doing what you love and what is right, even when others may be going down another path. It requires being willing to stand up for what you believe and to dance to your own beat when others are urging you to simply follow someone else's. It means being willing to take stands that may be unpopular and holding your ground.

Being true to yourself is the toughest principle to live by. Each of us is unique. It is up to you to determine who you are, who you want to become, and how you can best use the strengths and talents you were given to make a difference in the world. It helps to develop a thick skin. Many people judge others based on their occupation, their place of residence, and their friends. While this is all interesting information, it does not reveal whether a person is kind, helpful, or genuine.

Every once in a while, step back and reevaluate how you have grown and changed. The person you were ten years ago is not the person you are today. As you develop, have confidence in the person you are growing into. We believe that people can change—that's what this book is about. And once you've embraced change, your external actions will reflect the internal change. Don't be concerned about how others might perceive you; your actions will reveal the real you.

Arthur M. Blank, *cofounder of The Home Depot and owner and CEO of the Atlanta Falcons, talks about the importance of being true to yourself.*

~

Being true to yourself means sticking to your values—in business and in life. Our success at The Home Depot, for example, didn't happen by chance; it happened because we had a set of core values and made the very intentional choice to adhere to them. We always believed that American capitalism isn't just about money; it's also about meaning—connecting our deepest values to the work that we do by focusing on relationships rather than transactions, treating associates with respect and personal care, and giving back to our communities. It's a model I still try to follow today with all my businesses.

Arthur M. Blank is the owner and CEO of the Atlanta Falcons and the Georgia Force, and cofounder of The Home Depot. He is also the chairman, president, and CEO of AMB Group, LLC, and chairman of the Arthur M. Blank

Family Foundation. The foundation's purpose is to give back to society through financial contributions and personal involvement. Along with personal giving, the Blank Family Foundation has granted more than $250 million to support early childhood education, the arts, parks, and green space.

Rudy Giuliani, *former mayor of New York City, believes that sticking to your guns is more important than being popular.*

~

My hero is Ronald Reagan because he had strong beliefs and stuck to those beliefs. When Ronald Reagan ran for president in 1976, he did so by pursuing two core principles—making the federal government smaller and fighting communism. When that didn't win him the nomination, he didn't remake his philosophy. Ronald Reagan stuck to his guns and, by 1980, the country came around to embrace his point of view.

When I first ran for mayor, I adopted that approach and made my core principles smaller government, reducing taxes, improving quality of life, and fighting crime. As mayor, I applied those principles, even when they weren't popular, and I think the results show the value of developing strong beliefs and sticking to them.

Rudy Giuliani was mayor of New York City from 1994 through 2001. Prior to that, he was appointed by President Reagan as associate attorney general and then became the U.S. attorney for the southern district of New York. In recognition of his leadership during the attacks of September 11, he was named the 2001 Person of the Year by *Time* magazine.

Discovering Who You Are

Life is not easy for any of us. But what of that? We must have perseverance and, above all, confidence in ourselves. We must believe that we are gifted for something and that this thing must be attained.

—Marie Curie

Growing up, you try to please your parents, your teachers, your friends, and eventually your employers. We all work to measure up in others' eyes. But in the end, what others think of you is not important. What is important is what you have made of your gifts and talents, who you have become, and whether you have been true to yourself. The question is easy: What is the best way to be true to yourself? The answer is hard.

A strong sense of self is important for the times when others will try to influence your path. When you understand who you are and what values motivate you, it becomes easier to answer difficult questions and face challenges. If your highest priority is how best to fit in, you're going to have a tough time being true to yourself.

Jackie recalls a school lunch with her then second-grade daughter, Maggie, where Jackie was reminded that it is more important to be yourself than to fit in:

During lunch, I heard one of the students say, "I don't have to like the same things that you do. Friends can like different things."

That's one wise second grader, I thought. That was something I'd often told Maggie at home, and I was pleased she heard it at school as well. Sometimes children are smarter than we think!

We often go along to get along, or succumb to peer pressure. It's easier than fighting the crowd. But each time you give in against your better judgment, you lose a little bit of yourself. When you go along with other people's wishes at the expense of pursuing your own goals, you become what they wish rather than who you are supposed to be.

Of course, throughout your life, you will have to meet others halfway and cooperate in order to accomplish your dreams. Working together is often the best way to move rapidly, as long as your principles are not compromised.

But in the end, you have to recognize that your life's course is up to you. It's your responsibility to control it. As Molly Blank, a friend's grandmother, once told me, "You are born alone, and you die alone. Don't dump on anyone else for your decisions. You're a big girl, and you make them yourself."

It will take a good bit of self-examination and reflection to truly understand who *you* are as a person. While you may be influenced by your parents, teachers, family, and friends, you are unique. Every one of us has different strengths and weaknesses and different paths to fulfillment. Each member of our family is an individual who finds happiness in his or her own way. Your family too is made up of unique individuals. While we support one another and help one another grow, we are all different and have various talents, interests, and abilities.

Getting to know who you are requires spending quiet time looking inside yourself. Search for what you like to do, what your passions are, and what drives you to contribute. Pay attention to the world around you, and watch how you respond, interact, and behave in various situations. During this process, you might realize that some people see you in a different way from how you see yourself. That's okay. If you keep a clear focus on who you are and who you want to be, eventually others will begin to see you in the same light.

While you are determining who you are, you also need to determine who you want to become and what story you want your life to reflect when you are done. Imagine that you are ninety years old and talking to your great-grandchildren about your life. What story would you like to tell them?

Jackie talks about how one weekend with college friends inspired her to work toward her vision of her life:

We had graduated from college twenty years ago, but when the five of us went away for a weekend in the mountains, it felt as if we had not missed a beat. We were able to pick up, share stories, and laugh just the way we did in college. Three of us live in the Atlanta area, one lives in North Carolina, and the fifth (Ann Marie) flew in from Oregon.

Since she was coming from so far away, Ann Marie flew in the day before and spent the night at my home. Friends for more than two decades, we have been through a lot together. She's the type of friend I may not talk to for six months, but then when we talk, we'll pick up right where we left off. We brainstormed about what to do over our girls' weekend. Hiking and shopping were on our list. She suggested creating a vision board. As I am not the least bit artistic but am incredibly visual, this sounded like fun to me.

She gathered the poster board while I worked, and we bought dozens of magazines on the drive up from Atlanta. The next morning over coffee, we mentioned the idea to the rest of the group. There were a few skeptical remarks, but since it was raining, we decided to spend the morning on the project. Interestingly enough, after thirty minutes, we were all engrossed in the project of making a visual representation of how we wanted our lives to evolve. My vision board hangs in my office, right behind my computer in my line of sight. On days when I forget where I am going, I look and see my vision *of my future. It makes me work a bit harder and helps me focus my actions.*

No matter how old you are or what opportunities you might have missed along the way, the future really is yours. As George Eliot said, "It is never too late to be what you might have been." The rest of your life begins today. Each day you have a new opportunity to be true to yourself. That is why a key slogan in Alcoholics Anonymous is "One Day at a Time." For all of us, that is how life occurs. While your history might define who you *were,* your present determines who you *are,* and your future is your story to write.

Sharon Lechter, *coauthor of* Rich Dad Poor Dad *and the rest of the Rich Dad series of books, shares the importance of being true to yourself.*

~

Every major turning point in my life was a result of me being true to myself and to what I wanted out of my life. We all get so caught up in wanting to please other people that we often lose sight of what we truly want. Early in 2007, I realized that I was not being true to myself and my dream of teaching young people about money. As a result I made a significant change in my business life. This change was made for fulfillment of my life's purpose, not for money. I have never felt more true to myself!

My father always told me, "Make sure when you look in the mirror, you like who you see!"

Sharon L. Lechter is an entrepreneur, philanthropist, educator, CPA, international speaker, and mother. She is a lifelong education advocate and coauthor of the international bestselling book *Rich Dad Poor Dad* and the other books in the Rich Dad series. Lechter is also a founder and inventor of the CashFlow for Kids board game. She is launching a brand called YouthPreneur, which is designed to ignite children's entrepreneurial spirit. Lechter also serves on the President's Advisory Council on Financial Literacy.

Jackie Kallen, *one of the world's few women who promote professional boxing, notes that being true to herself took her down a path that offered few role models.*

~

When I first got into the boxing business, there were very few women involved. I was the only female boxing manager that I knew of. The men in the business tried to get me to dumb down and to act more like a man in order to fit in. I didn't care if I fit in. I wanted to be a success. And I would not trade my femininity or my own personal style. I did things *my* way— and it worked!

Jackie Kallen is one of the first and one of the most successful female boxing managers in history. She consults for the reality TV series *The Contender,* and Kallen's life is the inspiration for the film *Against the Ropes.*

Using Your Strengths

All of us attain the greatest success and happiness
possible in this life whenever we use our native
capacities to their fullest extent.

—Smiley Blanton, psychoanalyst

In their book *Now, Discover Your Strengths,* Marcus Buckingham and Donald Clifton cite voluminous research from the Gallup Organization to show readers how to identify their strengths and make the most of them. We all have strengths and weaknesses. While many management specialists focus on improving a person's weaknesses, Buckingham and Clifton take the opposite approach. They recommend focusing on our strengths as a more reliable recipe for success.

"Our fear of our weaknesses seems to overshadow our

confidence in our strengths," they write. Instead of relying on our strengths to pull us through, we allow our weaknesses to define our limits. Instead, we should focus on our strengths, stretching ourselves to use all of them.

When you focus on your weaknesses, you can become paralyzed, seeing only what is bad and ignoring what is good. By focusing instead on your strengths, you elbow aside any concerns about your weaknesses.

But what are your strengths? To answer that, ask yourself, What do I love to do? In general, we love doing what we are good at.

Ask your friends, peers, and colleagues what they see as your strengths. Since we only have our own view of the world, we may not even recognize talents in ourselves that may appear obvious to others. Asking for other people's perspectives can provide you with insight into strengths that you had not previously recognized. If you still don't have a clear idea of your strengths, take any of the numerous tests and inventories of skills that are available in bookstores or career centers.

It does not matter how you go about determining your strengths, as long as you do so. Once that is done, you can prepare to improve them.

Former UCLA basketball coach John Wooden, in his

autobiography, *Wooden: A Lifetime of Observations and Reflections On and Off the Court,* notes, "Many athletes have tremendous God-given gifts, but they don't focus on the development of those gifts. Who are these individuals? You've never heard of them—and you never will. It's true with sports and it's true everywhere in life."

You have to discover your strengths and focus on them. Yes, you have faults, too. Everyone does. But it is by determining your strengths and using them that you can set yourself apart and advance toward success. You can either be a mediocre someone else or an incredible you.

Once you have identified your strengths and begun to develop them, you will begin to perform at the edge of your ability. This will inevitably lead to failure in an area of strength. If you do not occasionally fail, then you are living in your comfort zone and will not grow your strengths. Some of us are afraid of failure, especially in our area of strength.

According to Buckingham and Clifton, the fear of failure can deter us from using our strengths. "Our sense of failure is most pervasive whenever we reach down [and] call upon our strengths, and they are found wanting," they write. While this may be painful, it provides a learning opportunity and allows for "strong living."

The hardest part of this process is accepting your weaknesses, accepting that you are not perfect, forgiving yourself, and beginning to focus on the areas where you excel—knowing all the while that you will fail but that doing so will ultimately help you develop your strengths.

Fearless living—living on the edge of your ability—will provide you with a lifetime of thrills.

Fox News Channel's legal correspondent Greta Van Susteren *talks about living on the edge and conquering life's adversities.*

⁓

Pursuit of these five principles is a must for success, but don't just stop with any one of them—go after each of them. Each is critical to success and not one is more important than another. Though pursuing each is not a guarantee for success, it's a great start. For complete personal success, you must also be ready for and able to conquer life's adversities. Adversity is inevitable. We all run into adversity. You may think you are the only one, but you are wrong. We all get it. Life is simply not perfect. But here is the secret: successful people face adversity head-on. . . . They feel appropriate pain from the disappointment but then pick themselves up, dust themselves off, and get going again. They overcome life's disappointments. If you can do that, you are unstoppable.

Greta Van Susteren joined Fox News Channel (FNC) in January 2002 as the host of the prime-time news and interview program *On the Record with Greta Van Susteren,* which launched in February 2002.

Prior to joining FNC, Van Susteren served as host of CNN's prime-time news and analysis show *The Point with Greta Van Susteren.* She also cohosted the network's daily legal program, *Burden of Proof.* Van Susteren joined CNN in 1991 as a legal analyst and, during her tenure with the network, contributed analysis to high-profile cases including the O. J. Simpson criminal and civil trials and the Elian Gonzalez custody battle. She also played an integral role in the legal analysis of CNN's coverage of Election 2000, for which she earned the American Bar Association's Presidential Award for Excellence in Journalism.

Recently dubbed one of the world's 100 Most Powerful Women by *Forbes* magazine, Van Susteren is the recipient of the 2000–2001 Sandra Day O'Connor Medal of Honor from Seton Hall University. She was also awarded the first-place 2002 National Headliners Award as part of an investigative team covering the "Attack on America."

In addition, Van Susteren is the coauthor of *My Turn at the Bully Pulpit: Straight Talk About the Things That Drive Me Nuts.*

Doing the Right Thing

The time is always right to do what is right.

—The Reverend Martin Luther King Jr.

There are two parts to "doing the right thing." The first is living with truth and honesty in your actions. While this is challenging enough, the second part is even harder: extending yourself and doing what you know should be done. It is taking that extra step and making the extra effort.

Truth and honesty form the starting point for doing the right thing. Cindi Seltzer Hoffman must have been shocked when she read "A Refugee from Gangland," a February 28, 2008, profile in the *New York Times*. It said that Margaret B. Jones, the author of *Love and Consequences,* was "a single mother who spent her youth as a foster child and gang member . . . dealing drugs on the streets of South Central LA."

Margaret B. Jones is a pseudonym for Margaret Seltzer, Cindi's sister.

Cindi knew that *Love and Consequences* was not a memoir but fiction. She called the publisher, Riverhead Books, an imprint of Penguin Group USA, and told the truth about the supposed memoir that had just launched to good reviews.

Within days, Riverhead Books had recalled all unsold copies of *Love and Consequences* and offered refunds to those who had already bought it. The publisher also canceled Seltzer's book tour.

Hoffman did what was true and right. She knew when she read the "memoir" that it was fiction.

Truth is easier to remember than fiction. The reason that lie detectors work is that the act of lying creates a physical reaction in your body: your pulse quickens, your blood pressure increases, and often you begin to sweat—all signs of stress. Clearly your body does not think that lying is good, so imagine what it might be doing to your soul. It is important not only to speak the truth but also to stand up for the truth when others are wrong.

Jackie recounts one such example:

It was the night that my boyfriend Jimmy (now my husband) met my dad. We went to Fado, an Irish pub in Atlanta. Both Dad and Jimmy like Guinness, and I thought that bonding over their mutual love of the Irish beer might be fun. Dad was Speaker of the House at the time, and going out with him meant quite a few stares and people pointing at and approaching us. It was crowded at Fado, and since the purpose of the night was for the two of them to get acquainted, I stood by myself a bit away from them. I could not help overhearing two men standing next to me, talking about Dad. One told the other, "There is Newt Gingrich. He abandoned his wife and children."

Now, it would have been easy to ignore what he had said, but it would not have been the right thing to do. He wasn't being mean, he was simply repeating incorrect information that he had heard somewhere. I leaned over and said, "Excuse me. He's my father and that's just not true." After being shocked for a moment, he apologized. The night was a success on two fronts: Dad and Jimmy became fast friends, and I have always been glad that I did the right thing by setting the record straight.

Doing the right thing requires not only honesty but also a willingness to take the right action—sometimes in a situation where it would be easier to stand back and do nothing. Theodore Roosevelt described it as living "the strenuous life."

Teedie, as his family called him, learned how to live strenuously when he was young. His first challenge was overcoming his physical limitations. He had severe asthma. On nights when the attacks were at their worst, his father would take him for rides in the night air to try to force air into his lungs.

When Teedie was about thirteen years old, his father told him, "You have the mind but you have not the body. You must make your body." His father had a gymnasium built in their home for the children to use. Though frail as a boy, Roosevelt was determined to overcome his limitations. He transformed himself by lifting weights and doing other exercises.

He was so successful that in 1898 he went on to serve in the cavalry as a Rough Rider. He became a hero after charging up San Juan and Kettle hills in Cuba.

While in his twenties, Roosevelt traveled to the Dakota Territory. There he lived the rugged outdoor life, learning to rope, ride, and survive in the wilderness. Roosevelt came to believe that the strong individualism of Americans was due, in part, to the western frontier. He also believed that without this western wilderness experience, he would never have become president.

Theodore Roosevelt came to believe that a full life was one that embraced tests, challenges, and growth. He gave a speech at the Hamilton Club in Chicago, in the spring of 1898, titled "The Strenuous Life."

"I wish to preach, not the doctrine of ignoble ease, but the doctrine of the strenuous life, the life of toil and effort, of labor and strife; to preach that highest form of success which comes, not to the man who desires mere easy peace, but to the man who does not shrink from danger, from hardship, or from bitter toil, and who out of these wins the splendid ultimate triumph."

This speech provided many arguments for working hard and overcoming adversity.

In addition, he said, a nation's health is linked to the health of its citizens:

In the last analysis a healthy state can exist only when the men and women who make it up can lead

clean, vigorous, healthy lives; when the children are
so trained that they shall endeavor, not to shirk dif-
ficulties, but to overcome them.

Roosevelt challenged individuals to search "not for the life of ease but for the life of strenuous endeavor." He lived out this idea in his own life, often hunting and riding, spending long stretches of time in the outdoors.

When President William McKinley died in 1901, Roosevelt became the nation's youngest president ever, at age forty-two. He became known as a reformer, a trust buster, and a conservationist. While president, he added more than 125 million acres of national forests and 51 bird sanctuaries. He truly led a strenuous life.

This idea of doing the right thing holds true for all areas of our lives—how we eat, exercise, treat people, and involve ourselves in our community.

While some might think that how you treat yourself is not important, that is simply not true. Your ability to be responsible to yourself, your family, your business, and your community is based on your ability to respond to their needs. You can respond to others' needs only after your own basic needs have been met. Making sure that you get enough sleep and exercise and that you eat right prepares you to be responsible when you need to be.

Newt remembers talking to Bo Callaway in 1970 about Bo's very disciplined exercise schedule. "I am amazed you can always work exercise into your day," Newt told the businessman and former politician from Georgia as the two men walked together.

Callaway stopped walking and turned to Newt. "You know, until now I thought we both had the same twenty-four hours in a day. It never occurred to me I had more hours than you did." It was a lesson in setting priorities that Newt never forgot.

If all this appears a bit overwhelming, remember that we all have reserves of energy and spirit within us that enable us to do more than we might think possible. As Christopher Robin told Winnie the Pooh, "Promise me you'll always remember: You're braver than you believe, and stronger than you seem, and smarter than you think."

Doing the right thing may sound easy, but it is hard. It requires knowing the right thing to do, mustering the discipline to do it, and finding the ability to forgive yourself when you fail. Doing the right thing means using all the strengths and opportunities that you are given in such a way that it will improve the world.

Richard DeVos *talks about the importance of being true to yourself, in all areas of life.*

⁓

It's not always easy, but it's very important to be true to yourself. However, to be true to yourself you need to know deep in your heart what you really believe. What are the values that guide you? What does your faith teach you to be true to? As for me, I am a Christian, and my faith helps me a lot in knowing what is best for me. It helps me make decisions in both my work life and my home life. It doesn't mean I don't have questions or struggles, but it does make a whole lot of issues clearer and decisions easier.

In 2006, I was a candidate for governor of Michigan. Many people wanted me to change my beliefs just so I would have a better chance of getting elected. So I had to decide if being true to myself or winning an election was more important, and being true to myself won. And ultimately I lost the election. But you know the good news? The day after I lost I still felt great, because I knew I had stayed true to myself.

Richard DeVos is president of the Windquest Group, a multicompany management group involved in the manufacture and marketing of storage and space-utilization products. He is the former president of Alticor Inc., was president and CEO of the Orlando Magic basketball franchise from 1991 to 1993, and was the Republican nominee for governor of Michigan in 2006.

Atlanta mayor Shirley Franklin *talks about the importance of public officials doing the right thing the right way.*

⁓

A s public officials, we find that our most lasting contributions are not always what we did but *how* we did it.

It is important to me that the public and voters know that I feel a sense of responsibility to be transparent, to be accountable, to make data-driven decisions, and to do my best every day.

Values are learned, and my parents were my first instructors. My mother's early advice was to do my best. My father taught me the joy of a rigorous commitment to intellectual pursuit. And finally, as someone who came to public office later in life, I have learned the value of finding my own voice. I frequently encourage young women to find their passion, their voice, and their destinies in unexpected and unlikely opportunities.

Shirley Franklin was fifty-six years old in 2001 when she was elected mayor of Atlanta as a first-time candidate. With her victory, she became the first woman to hold the job and the first African-American woman to serve as mayor of any major Southern city. Mayor Franklin has worked since her inauguration in 2002 to build a "Best in Class" managed city by strengthening existing frameworks, implementing changes, and making the tough decisions necessary to improve Atlanta.

Julie Gerberding, *former Centers for Disease Control and Prevention director, talks about being true in your performance.*

~

Trust in government has never been more critical to our nation, and making trust the final indicator of success is the only way I can stay true to myself. For me, trust is a function of the three T's—truth, transparency, and transaction. In other words, speaking honestly, opening decisions for broad input and debate, and doing what you say you will do. All are necessary, but truth-telling has been the foundation on which I have based all tough decisions at CDC (Centers for Disease Control and Prevention). In times of national emergency, people need to have the truth from CDC—what we know, what we don't know, and what we are doing to help. Likewise, when controversial policies are debated, people need to have the whole truth about the science underlying CDC's recommendations, even when they exercise their freedom to debate how values and political realities should influence the ultimate decision.

Julie Louise Gerberding became the director of the Centers for Disease Control and Prevention in July 2002 in the wake of the terrorism attacks on our nation. Under her leadership, CDC dramatically expanded its domestic and international reach, enhanced public health preparedness for emerging threats like SARS and pandemic influenza, and established public health goals that target the health threats that prevent America from being a "Healthiest Nation."

General Peter Pace, USMC *(Retired), the sixteenth chairman of the Joint Chiefs of Staff, relates a story of the importance of facing moral challenges with the correct response.*

⁓

In my forty years in uniform, I'm most proud of my time as a rifle platoon leader in Vietnam. That's where I learned the most important lesson of my life: Be true to yourself by checking your moral compass.

We were on patrol and one of my Marines was killed by a sniper. A sense of rage filled me and I started to call in an artillery strike on the village from which the bullet had been fired. My platoon sergeant didn't say anything—he just looked at me. I knew by his look that what I was doing was wrong.

I called off the artillery strike, and we did what we should have done, which was to walk through the village, where we found nothing but women and children. Had that artillery strike been conducted, I don't know how I could possibly have lived with myself.

What I learned that day I've used every day thereafter, and not just in combat.

Check your moral compass. Think through what might happen, whether it has to do with taking a test in school or working in a business that handles a lot of money or meeting with people who have different ideas.

All of us face moral challenges. If you have not thought through who you want to be at the end of each day, you may not like the person you end up being.

General Peter Pace has served for more than forty years in the United States Marine Corps. His accomplishments include serving as vice chairman and then as sixteenth chairman of the Joint Chiefs of Staff (the first marine to have held either of these positions), the principal military adviser to the president and the secretary of defense, and filling roles in the National Security Council and the Homeland Security Council.

Being Authentic

The highest courage is to dare to appear to be what one is.

—Bishop John Lancaster Spalding

From plastic plants to fake fur, we are surrounded by imitations—some good, some not so good. This movement away from authenticity has come about for a variety of reasons, including lower cost (polyester versus silk), reduced maintenance requirements (plastic plants versus real ones), and in some cases, a belief in not causing harm (fake fur versus real pelts).

While such replacements might mean less monetary cost, less upkeep, or increased durability, there is normally a trade-off. It might be easier to take care of a silk version of a stargazer lily, but the replacement flower lacks the fragrance of the real thing.

Every day, each of us makes trade-offs between benefit and cost in numerous personal decisions. Authenticity requires you to focus on core beliefs and to stand firm amid changing events over which you may have no control. If we are looking for authenticity, we should first define what it means to be authentic. The Merriam-Webster online dictionary defines the adjective "authentic" as "worthy of acceptance or belief as conforming to or based on fact . . . true to one's own personality, spirit, or character."

To be authentic, we must line up what we think, say, and do so that they are all in agreement—an almost impossible task. While occasionally we will fail, make mistakes, and contradict ourselves, it is important for us to acknowledge our failings with the goal of becoming more authentic.

Authenticity means knowing who we are and striving to be that person in every situation while treating others with respect. After all, if we know who we are, and we are authentic, we have nothing we need to prove. It means being true to ourselves.

The way we act influences not only what others think of us but also, more important, what we think of ourselves. In *Developing the Leader Within You*, John C.

Maxwell talks about the importance of integrity, "when my words and my deeds match up." According to Maxwell, "a person with integrity does not have divided loyalties (that's duplicity), nor is he or she merely pretending (that's hypocrisy). People with integrity are 'whole' people; they can be identified by their single-mindedness. People with integrity have nothing to hide and nothing to fear. Their lives are open books." Integrity provides you with credibility as a person. People begin to understand that what you are and how you act are linked: they trust what you say and understand your actions.

Authenticity is hard to achieve, because it requires that you be brutally honest in exposing to others your weaknesses, failings, and faults along with your strengths and achievements. Allowing yourself to be vulnerable requires great strength.

The father of our country knew this. George Washington used his authenticity to turn around a contentious meeting at a delicate time in our nation's history. It was March 1783. The English had surrendered at Yorktown in October 1781, but the British soldiers continued to occupy New York while the peace treaty was being negotiated. The soldiers in the Continental Congress were exhausted and frustrated. Their pay had fallen behind, and the army was having problems supplying them with food and clothing. Imagine you're a soldier, you have won the war for your new country, but more than a year later you are cold, hungry, and broke. A group of disgruntled soldiers began to discuss mutiny. On March 15, 1783, Washington met with the rebellious officers in an attempt to ease the tension. Washington was the man who had led the army to victory. The men adored him, and many talked of making him king of the new country. As he walked into the room, he had every man's attention. What would he say?

He began with a plea for order and democracy, noting that he did not want to be king. His words appeared to fall on deaf ears; the soldiers were angry and upset. He appealed to them to do what was right, but this elicited no reaction. Washington then pulled out a letter he had received from a congressman asking him to relay his support to the soldiers, but Washington could not read the letter.

There was tension in the room as the soldiers watched Washington pull out his glasses. "Gentlemen, you will permit me to put on my spectacles," he said, "for I have not only grown gray but almost blind in the service of my country." This totally disarmed the soldiers. How could they complain about their status when their commander-in-chief had almost lost his sight? Their sacrifice seemed small in comparison.

Washington's ability to express his authenticity and show his weakness proved to be a strength. It changed the dynamic of the meeting with the potentially mutinous soldiers, and perhaps the destiny of our nation.

Being authentic is a daily endeavor and requires that you pay attention to who you really are and who you are becoming. Remember that you get to determine where and with what degree of authenticity and integrity you will live. As the Reverend Martin Luther King Jr. stated, "There is always time to do what is right." Take the time and live your life right. There is plenty of time—but you only have one life.

Being true to yourself is the last of the five principles—and the hardest to master. It is the one you will have to work at the most, but it will give you the most satisfaction and will ensure that you have mastered the four other principles so that you are following your life's purpose.

Living a successful life is living the life that only you can live. We all have the spark of the divine in us. It is up to each of us to find that spark, nurture it, and allow it to shine brightly, while encouraging others in their journeys through life. As Nelson Mandela said:

> *Our deepest fear is not that we are inadequate. Our deepest fear is that we are powerful beyond measure. It is our light, not our darkness, that most frightens us. We ask ourselves, who am I to be brilliant, gorgeous, talented, and fabulous? Actually, who are you not to be? You are a child of God! Your playing small doesn't serve the world. There's nothing enlightened about shrinking so that other people won't feel insecure around you. We were born to make manifest the glory of God that is within us. It's not just in some of us; it is in everyone. And as we let our own light shine, we unconsciously give other people permission to do the same. As we are liberated from our own fear, our presence automatically liberates others.*

Liberate yourself from your fear of inadequacy, remind yourself daily that you are a glorious child of God, here to live your best life.

Dream big, work hard, learn every day, enjoy life, be true to yourself—and live a successful life.

Acknowledgments

Special thanks to Callista Gingrich and Jimmy Cushman Jr., for their constant support, love, and encouragement.

This book has been made possible due to the dedication and help of many people.

We would like to thank Counts and Associates, Crown Publishing, Cushman Enterprises, Gingrich Communications, the Lubbers Agency, McKenna Long & Aldridge, the Office of Speaker Newt Gingrich, and those who have made this book possible, including: Ben Bartlett, Mary Choteborsky, Cynthia Counts, Joe DeSantis, Randy Evans, Steve Hanser, Sonya Harrison, Lindsey Harvey, Kathy Lubbers, Kim Mallen, Anthony Morris, Michelle Selesky, Whitney Smith, and Rick Tyler.

Jackie wants to specially acknowledge her mother, Jackie Gingrich, for her role in making this book a reality. Jackie thanks Tom Watkins, for his advice, edits, and encouragement; Sam Candler, Rayna Casey, Caroline Davis, and Thornton Kennedy, for their help and encouragement.

Thank you to the Learning Makes a Difference Foundation and the Learn and Earn Team, including: Adell Atwood, Ramsay Battin, Nancy Blank, Kirsten Boehner,

Drevyeel Cunningham, Vicki Denmark, Jim Emshoff, Lori Fanning, Greg Fields, Darron Franklin, the Fulton County School Board, Stanley King, Lashaunda Latham, Cindy Loe, Charlie Loudermilk, David Mackey, Connie Maggert, Latrelle McFarlane, Ericka Montag, Robb Pitts, Michael Robinson, Karol Stephens, Dewitt Walker, Heather White, Kirk Wilks, and James Wilson.

Finally, we appreciate the active participation of those who contributed their personal quotes, which truly enhanced this project: John Abizaid, Arthur Blank, John Bolton, Tom Brokaw, Jeb Bush, Tucker Carlson, James Carville, Jim Clifton, Bill Clinton, Alan Colmes, Dick DeVos, Shirley Franklin, Carly Fiorina, Julie Gerberding, Edmund Giambastiani, Rudy Giuliani, Whoopi Goldberg, Ricardo González, Luis Haza, Lou Holtz, Jack Horner, Jackie Kallen, Patrick Kerney, Sharon Lechter, Rush Limbaugh, Jim Loehr, Jill Long, Bernie Marcus, Mary Matalin, Oliver North, John Ondrasik, Bill O'Reilly, Peter Pace, Tom Peters, David Petraeus, Michael Reagan, Tavis Smiley, James Stavridis, Michael Steele, Jon Stewart, Greta Van Susteren, and John Williams. We are grateful they took the time to inspire others.

Recommended Reading

Authentic Happiness: Using the New Positive Psychology to Realize Your Potential for Lasting Fulfillment. Martin E. P. Seligman, Ph.D. New York: Free Press, 2002.

Building Leaders the West Point Way: Ten Principles from the Nation's Most Powerful Leadership Lab. Major General Joseph P. Franklin, U.S. Army (retired). Nashville: Thomas Nelson, 2007.

The Effective Executive. Peter F. Drucker. New York: HarperBusiness, 1993.

Finding Flow: The Psychology of Engagement with Everyday Life. Mihaly Csikszentmihalyi. New York: Basic Books, 1997.

First, Break All the Rules: What the World's Greatest Managers Do Differently. Marcus Buckingham and Curt Coffman. New York: Simon & Schuster, 1999.

Gross National Happiness: Why Happiness Matters for America—and How We Can Get More of It. Arthur C. Brooks. New York: Basic Books, 2008.

If You Want to Walk on Water, You've Got to Get Out of the Boat. John Ortberg. Grand Rapids, Michigan: Zondervan, 2001.

Learned Optimism: How to Change Your Mind and Your Life. Martin E. P. Seligman, Ph.D. New York: Vintage Books, 2006.

The Magic of Thinking Big. David J. Schwartz, Ph.D. New York: Fireside, 2007.

Mindfulness. Ellen J. Langer. Reading, Mass.: Addison-Wesley, 1989.

Mindset: The New Psychology of Success. Carol Dweck. New York: Random House, 2006.

Now, Discover Your Strengths. Marcus Buckingham and Donald Clifton. New York: Free Press, 2001.

The Power of Kindness: The Unexpected Benefits of Leading a Compassionate Life. Piero Ferrucci. New York: Penguin, 2006.

The Power of Positive Thinking. Norman Vincent Peale. New York: Fireside, 2003.

The Power of Story: Rewrite Your Destiny in Business and in Life. Jim Loehr. New York: Free Press, 2007.

The Seven Habits of Highly Effective People: Restoring the Character Ethic. Stephen R. Covey. New York: Fireside, 1990.

The Spontaneous Fulfillment of Desire: Harnessing the Infinite Power of Coincidence. Deepak Chopra. New York: Three Rivers Press, 2003.

Stress for Success: The Proven Program for Transforming

Stress into Positive Energy at Work. James Loehr. New York: Three Rivers Press, 1997.

The Success Principles™: How to Get from Where You Are to Where You Want to Be. Jack Canfield with Janet Switzer. New York: HarperCollins, 2005.

Thank You Power: Making the Science of Gratitude Work for You. Deborah Norville. Nashville: Thomas Nelson, 2007.

True North: Discover Your Authentic Leadership. Bill George with Peter Sims. San Francisco: Jossey-Bass, 2007.

You Are the Message: Secrets of the Master Communicators. Roger Ailes with Jon Kraushar. New York: Doubleday, 1989.

Walt Disney: The Triumph of the American Imagination. Neal Gabler. New York: Knopf, 2006.

Who Really Cares: The Surprising Truth About Compassionate Conservatism; America's Charity Divide—Who Gives, Who Doesn't, and Why It Matters. Arthur C. Brooks, New York: Basic Books, 2006.

Wooden: A Lifetime of Observations and Reflections On and Off the Court. Coach John Wooden with Steve Jamison. New York: McGraw-Hill, 1997.

Photography Credits

John Bolton courtesy of Washington Speakers Bureau
Tom Brokaw courtesy of NBC News
Jeb Bush courtesy of Washington Speakers Bureau
Tucker Carlson courtesy of NBC
Jim Clifton courtesy of James K. Clifton
Bill Clinton by Ralph Alswang/Clinton Foundation
Alan Colmes courtesy of Fox News Channel
Whoopi Goldberg by Timothy White
Luis Haza courtesy of Luis Haza
Lou Holtz courtesy of Louis Holtz
Jack Horner by Celeste Horner
Jackie Kallen courtesy of Hilary Lidestri
Patrick Kerney courtesy of Corky Trewin/Seattle Seahawks
Sharon Lechter courtesy of Sharon L. Lechter
Jim Loehr courtesy of Jim Loehr
Oliver North by Andrew Stenner for Fox News
John Ondrasik courtesy of Jim Wright
General Peter Pace courtesy of Peter Pace
Tom Peters courtesy of Allison Shirreffs
General David Petraeus by SSG Lorie Jewell, courtesy of the
    U.S. Army
Tavis Smiley courtesy of Tavis Smiley
Jon Stewart by Norman Jean Roy
Greta Van Susteren courtesy of Fox News Channel